THE REAL SOLUTION ANGER CONTROL WORKBOOK

Richard Pfeiffer, M.Div. CGP

GROWTH PUBLISHING
NEW YORK

THE
REAL SOLUTION
ANGER
CONTROL
WORKBOOK

COPYRIGHT © 1998 RICHARD H PFEIFFER

-ALL RIGHTS RESERVED-

NO PART OF THIS BOOK MAY BE REPRODUCED OR TRANSMITTED
IN ANY FORM OR BY ANY MEANS, ELECTRONIC OR MECHANICAL,
INCLUDING PHOTOCOPYING, RECORDING, OR BY ANY INFORMATION
STORAGE AND RETRIEVAL SYSTEM,
WITHOUT PERMISSION IN WRITING FROM THE PUBLISHER

PRINTED IN THE UNITED STATES OF AMERICA

FIRST EDITION

SECOND PRINTING

ISBN 1893505006

GROWTH PUBLISHING
DIVISION OF GROWTH GROUPS
750 COLUMBUS AVENUE
SUITE 9S
NEW YORK, NY 10025
http://growthgroups.com

PREFACE

I owe The Real Solution Anger Control Workbook to fifteen years of conversation with extraordinary men and women. Under the outward roles of therapist and client, student and teacher, or colleague and colleague, in order to first make human connection, many individuals have impacted this work. I want to express my gratitude to those who have influenced this book.

I first want to thank my wife Dr. Anita Bohensky for the support and love that has truly been the catalyst for The Real Solution Workbooks. Her caring and thoughtful way has taught me more about the integration of affect and intellect than she can ever know.

I want to express appreciation to my daughter Sara for her help in editing, organizing, and sometimes stretching me in my personal understanding of the material. I want to thank my stepdaughter Megan for her editing and helpful suggestions along the way. I have also very much appreciated the support and listening ears given to me by my daughter Rebecca and stepdaughter Erin.

I am grateful to my colleagues at the Creative Living Counseling Center for their sharing of themselves and understandings in this work that we do, especially: Dr. Dan Bottorff, Dr. Marilyn Batchelder, Dr. James Wyrtzen, Dr. Gretchen Janssen, Elizabeth Ehling, M.Div., Shirley Gilliam, M.Div., Marcia Wyrtzen, LCSW, Constance Ritzler, MA, Dr. Yvonne Martinez Thorne, Dr. Leo Samouilidis, and of course Kathy Corniotes.

I would also like to acknowledge those who I first connected with at Blanton-Peale Graduate Institute and who have certainly influenced this work including: Dr. Wilbert Sykes, Dr. Bert Weinblatt, Dr. Herb Rabin, Dr. Margaret Kornfeld, Dr. John McNeill, Dr. James Murphy, Dr. Dustin Nichols, Steve Prichard, M.Div., Dr. Robert Thorne, and Carrol Arkema, M.Div.

Richard H Pfeiffer

2

Using the Workbook

The best predictor of a positive outcome is your willingness to honestly examine and admit the consequences of your anger problem. Because The Real Solution Anger Control Workbook requires a great deal of compliance in the form of assignments, exercises, homework and self-monitoring, you will need to be motivated. Think for a moment what your anger has cost you in terms of your relationships, health, work life, and financial situation.

The Workbook is organized to complete one session per week. You need to make a commitment in advance to set aside time for the entire twelve sessions of the Workbook. Stick with it and discuss your dissatisfactions with a trusted friend instead of dropping out. Because the Workbook's focus is on developing skills, and each new skill relies to some extent on what has previously been learned, you will need to do the sessions in sequence. It is best to do one session per week, however you may complete the sessions at a faster pace without significant consequences. Completion of this Workbook will pay off in many ways.

4

CONTENTS

PREFACE	1
USING THE WORKBOOK	3
CONTENTS	5
SESSION ONE	9
Getting Started	11
Clarifying Expectations	11
The Miracle Day Exercise	13
The Anger Log	15
SESSION TWO	17
Review of Previous Session	19
The Shame Problem	19
Assessment	20
Surviving Shame	21
Denial	21
Withdrawal	22
Anger Is a Two-Part Process	23
Ventilation Doesn't Work	23
Anger Is Different From Aggression	24
Coping is Better Than Blaming	24
SESSION THREE	25
The Shame Problem	27
Review: Survival Strategies for Shame	27
Surviving Shame	28
Perfectionism	28
Rage	29
Progressive Muscle Relaxation	31
Relaxation Without Tension	32
Special Place Visualization	33
Breathing-Cued Relaxation	34
Cue-Controlled Relaxation	34
Combined Relaxation	34
Cognitive Control/Relaxation Training	35

SESSION FOUR   39

    The Shame Problem   41

      Surviving Shame   41

       Arrogance   42

       Exhibitionism   43

    More Coping Skills Rehearsal   44

    ABC Cognitive Theory   45

    Trigger Thoughts   47

      Shoulds   47

      Entitlement   48

      Fairness   49

      Global labeling   50

    Coping Statements For Trigger Thoughts   50

      General Coping Thoughts and Strategies   51

SESSION FIVE   53

    The Shame Problem   55

      Significant Problems Associated with Shame   55

       Shame and the Self Centered Universe   55

       Shame and the Fear of Abandonment   55

       "I Will Be Whatever You Want Me to Be"   56

       Self Sabotage   56

       Self Abuse   56

       Self Neglect   56

       The Tendency to Humiliate Others   57

       Compulsive/Addictive Behaviors   57

    More Coping Skills Rehearsal   58

    Coping Skills Rehearsal   58

SESSION SIX   61

    The Shame Problem   63

      Current Shaming Relationships   63

    More Coping Skills Rehearsal   65

    Coping in the Scene II   65

SESSION SEVEN	67
The Shame Problem	69
Shaming Yourself	69
Description of Response Choice Rehearsal	71
Response Choice Rehearsal*	71
Active Responses	72
Passive Responses	72
First RCR *Response: Ask for What You Want*	74
Rules	74
Role Play	75
SESSION EIGHT	77
Healing the Shame	79
Stage One: Understanding	79
Patience – Healing Shame is a Process	79
Full Awareness of Your Shame	80
Explore Your Defenses Against Shame	81
Explore the Sources of Your Shame	81
Accept your Shame as Part of the Human Condition	82
Review Homework	82
Second RCR *Response: Negotiate*	83
Rules	83
Role Play	83
Third RCR *Response: Self-Care*	84
Rules	84
SESSION NINE	87
Healing the Shame	89
The Action Stage	89
Get help – you don't have to do this alone	90
Challenge the shame	91
Set positive goals based on:	91
The Principle of Humanity	91
The Principle of Humility	91
The Principle of Autonomy	92
The Principle of Competence	92
Take mental and physical action to move toward those goals	92
Fourth RCR *Response: Get Information*	93
Fifth RCR *Response: Acknowledge*	93
Sixth RCR *Response: Withdrawal*	94

SESSION TEN	97
Healing the Shame	99
From the Family of Origin	99
Difference between exploring the past & getting stuck in it	100
Deficiency messages you received from your family	100
Grieve your life losses resulting from these messages	101
Review Homework	102
RCR Switching	102
Role-Play	103

SESSION ELEVEN	107
Healing the Shame	109
From the Family of Origin	109
Challenge the old deficiency messages and replace with positive new ones	109
Challenge Exercise	110
Challenge your behavior so it is consistent with self-worth	111
Review Homework	111
More RCR Switching	112
Review *Role-Play*	112
Expressing Negative Emotion - Saying "No"	113

SESSION TWELVE	
Healing the Shame	115
From the Family of Origin	117
Return 'borrowed shame'	117
Consider forgiving so you can be released from shame	117
Review Homework: Saying "No"	119
Relapses	120
A New Beginning	121
Evaluation	122

ABOUT THE AUTHOR	123

APPENDIX	125

SESSION ONE

Getting Started

Clarifying Expectations

The Miracle Day Exercise

The Anger Log

Homework

Getting Started

You have a lot to cover in this Workbook. You're going to have some fun, but you're also going to have to work pretty hard. You can achieve several things: you can learn to reduce levels of anger especially in provocative situations, you can learn some effective coping skills in order to halt escalation and to resolve conflicts, and you can learn and understand about the role of shame in your life as well as enhance your self-concept. There will be homework to do, and you will begin practicing what you've learned in real situations. Most of your time will be spent learning new skills and then practicing them. There's a lot for you to do. So roll up your sleeves and let's get started.

Clarifying Expectations

Take a little time here at the beginning of your work to think about some of the things you're hoping to get out of doing this Workbook. There are no right or wrong answers to this - please try not to leave out anything, even if you think it might be unreasonable. If they're your ideas, they are of value.

It's natural to come to the Workbook feeling either hopeful or hopeless. Anger Control problems develop over a long period of time, and you may have been angry for many years. Your problem is unlikely to disappear over night. What you will do in a later session is work to develop realistic and manageable short-term goals that may or may not be symptom-related.

As a person with anger problems you may frequently find yourself setting unrealistic goals and standards for yourself. This tendency to be hard on yourself may appear as you set overly ambitious goals for change and growth in this Workbook. Change and growth are not about *all or nothing,* there is such a thing as *some* change and *some* growth and it is a process that takes *some* time. It is important to remind yourself frequently of this tendency of being hard on yourself and remind yourself that the recovery process is one that will begin with this Workbook but will continue long after it is completed.

List Four Overall Goals you have for doing this Workbook:

1.

2.

3.

4.

Miracle Day Exercise

The first exercise you will do is an 'imagination' exercise. Please read all the questions and answer them as completely as you can, including as many specific details as possible. Consider how your feelings (internal experiences) and your actions (external behaviors) would be different from what they are now.

When completing the question regarding your miracle day, it is important to include both how you will feel different and (as a result) what you would do differently or what others would observe as different about you.

Take some time now to complete all the questions.

1. Imagine that when you go to sleep tonight, sometime during the night while you are sleeping, a miracle occurs. All the problems that brought you to The Real Solution Assertiveness Workbook are solved. When you wake up tomorrow, what would your "miracle day" be like? (Describe this miracle day with as much specific detail as you can.)

2. Who would be the first person to notice something different about you? What would he or she notice? (Remember that people cannot see your internal experiences. Focus on what he or she would observe that is different in your behaviors.)

3. Who else would notice something different about you? What would these individuals notice?

4. If no one else would notice something different about you, what would you notice different about yourself?

5. Using the following scale, with 10 being your miracle day and 1 being the furthest away from your miracle day, what is the closest to your miracle day you have ever gotten in the last year?

1	5	10

6. Describe the time identified in the previous question in detail. Include whom you were with, what he or she noticed that was different about you, when it was and where you were, and what you were doing and why you were doing it.

7. Using the same scale (10 is your miracle day, 1 is furthest away from your miracle day) where are you today?

1	5	10

The Anger Log

The log is an indispensable tool for self-observation, facilitating change, and monitoring progress. An anger log entry should include the date and time, the situation, anger-triggering thoughts, emotional arousal (rated on a one-to-ten scale), and aggressive behavior (rated on a one-to-ten scale). Use the Anger log to record times when you feel angry in the coming weeks. (Go to pg. 16)

DATE/TIME	SITUATION	TRIGGER THOUGHTS	EMOTIONAL AROUSAL Scale: 1-10	AGGRESSIVE BEHAVIOR Scale: 1-10

Homework
- Daily monitoring of angry feelings this week through the anger log.

SESSION TWO

Review of Previous Session

The Shame Problem

Assessment

Surviving Shame

Anger Is a Two-Part Process

Ventilation Doesn't Work

Anger Is Different From Aggression

Coping is Better Than Blaming

Homework

Review of Previous Session

The "pink cloud" phenomenon, a sort of euphoria about your anticipated recovery without taking account of the hard work that will be involved or the inevitable setbacks you'll encounter along the way, may last for the first few sessions. Or maybe you are having some negative reactions to the material. It is important that you talk to someone about any 'bad' feelings you are experiencing with this Workbook. Things will get a little rougher, as you go along. It will pay off to hang in through the rough times toward completion.

Go over your Anger Log. Did you notice any patterns about your anger?

The Problem with Shame

Most people can stand up to normal, temporary shame. That kind of shame certainly hurts, but it will eventually disappear. Good shame provides messages we need to hear. But, for persons who live with excessive shame, shame never seems to go away, no matter what they do. If they listened to it all the time, they might be driven to take desperate action or just give up in despair. This shame often seems too painful to endure.

Healthy and Unhealthy Shame

Shame and guilt can sometimes be confused. Guilt is when we have done something wrong. Shame is when we *are* something wrong. Shame is a universal experience and everyone has shame to some degree. It can be healthy or unhealthy. Healthy shame is normal, temporary, and provides messages for us that maintain a healthy balance for our thinking and behavior. Unhealthy shame is excessive and distorted. We have been shamed more than normal either by prolonged or repeated, perhaps chronic events. Excessive shame doesn't seem to ever go away.

Assessment

Fill out the following Shame Assessment. You will probably have some high numbers in some area and low ones in others. This self-assessment is meant for you to use to begin to think about and understand more of the role of shame in you life.

On a scale of 0 - 10 (with 0 being <u>not at all</u> and 10 being <u>severe</u>) How would you rate yourself?	1	2	3	4	5	6	7	8	9	10
I WORRY ABOUT HOW I LOOK										
I AM CONCERNED ABOUT WHAT OTHERS THINK OF ME										
WHEN I TALK ABOUT WHAT I REALLY THINK, I'M EMBARRASSED LATER										
I FEEL SELF-CONSCIOUS WHEN I'M WITH OTHERS										
I HAVE TROUBLE HANDLING CRITICISM										
I'M AFRAID I'LL BE HUMILIATED IN FRONT OF OTHERS										
I EXPECT OTHERS TO SEE MY FLAWS										
I NOTICE MY OWN FLAWS AND FAULTS DAILY										
WHEN OTHERS PRAISE ME, IT'S HARD FOR ME TO BELIEVE WHAT THEY'RE SAYING										
I DON'T THINK I'M AS GOOD AS OTHER PEOPLE I KNOW										
I FEEL SHAME ABOUT THE WAY OTHER PEOPLE IN MY FAMILY ACT										
SOMETIMES I FEEL ASHAMED AND I DON'T KNOW WHY										
I WORRY ABOUT WHAT I'LL DO WRONG										
I HATE BEING EVALUATED, EVEN THOUGH I KNOW I HAVE DONE A GOOD JOB										
I FEEL SHAME JUST BEING NEAR SOMEBODY WHO'S ACTING DUMB.										

Survival Strategies for Shame

There are several ways people distort their shame feelings. The people who repress shame may not even be aware that they are defending themselves against feelings of shame. They may not even recognize shame as the problem.

Defenses against shame may help a person deal with feelings of self-hatred and pain, but in the long run they do not heal shame. No one can learn to benefit from shame by ignoring it. Defenses against shame are survival strategies only; excessively shamed individuals who use them cannot learn that they are valuable persons who are worthy of love and respect. The first two defenses against shame will be discussed in this session.

Denial

The first kind of defense is denial. Someone who is in denial simply stays unaware of his shame. He deceives himself into believing he has no shame, when, in fact, he would experience great shame if he were fully aware of what was happening inside. He badly wants to believe he is completely acceptable to himself and to others, and so he blinds himself to whatever would bring him shame.

The people who are excessively shamed often live in a world of appearances. They will do anything to protect their image as a good person, even if that means ignoring reality. For example, many alcoholics deny their drinking problem. They would feel tremendous shame if they admitted they couldn't control their alcohol use. They believe something must be wrong with anyone who is powerless over a mere bottle. They cannot understand how someone could be both an alcoholic and a good person at the same time. They believe: *An alcoholic is a worthless bum. I'm not that way. I'd hate myself if I were a drunk. I can't be an alcoholic.* Their fear of overwhelming shame is so strong they are blinded to the evidence of addiction. These people cannot face their shame, so they convince themselves there is no problem.

Denial of shame is not exclusive to alcoholics. After all, shame threatens the core identity of a person. Whatever could bring shame to someone can be defended against with denial. We defend against what we

21

dare not see. Living in denial however takes its toll on a person. Slips of anger control can cause lots of problems. It is primary in recovery to face reality even when it is excruciatingly painful. But you can only do that when you learn that you can survive your shame. The way out of shame is to come out of hiding.

Can you think of anyone who uses denial as a defense? Is there a part of you that can use this defense? How did you learn it?

Withdrawal

Another survival strategy against shame is withdrawal. People withdraw when they have been touched by shame, and personal contact with others is too painful to handle. Flight is a normal reaction to situations when people feel exposed and vulnerable. Withdrawal is a common reaction to shame. Remember that the initial physical reaction to shame is to break eye contact and look down or aside. A person who is shamed more or less says to his companions: *Right now I feel so bad about myself that I cannot look you in the eye. I can't stay close to you because that will only increase my shame.* Already feeling naked before the world, a person who is excessively shamed certainly doesn't want another person to stare at him. He believes, at least temporarily, that everyone can see his soul, see that he is inadequate and bad.

Persons who are excessively shamed also withdraw in other ways. Perhaps they evade uncomfortable topics of conversation or stay emotionally unavailable to others. Some persons practice the art of low visibility. They are always there, but not visible. One example is the very talented person behind the scenes who is so afraid of exposure that he lets others take credit for his accomplishments.

A person who is excessively shamed can become trapped in the withdrawal from others. He may do anything to keep others distant, as if they had already shamed him. Direct, meaningful, or intimate connections to others are very threatening to people who do not feel good about themselves. 'Not feeling good about yourself' is code for shame. Keeping others distant is a protection from the humiliation of being judged or rejected.

Can you think of anyone who uses withdrawal as a defense? Is there a part of you that can use this defense? How did you learn it?

Anger Is a Two-Part Process

Anger starts with the experience of pain. The pain can be physical or emotional: it can be a stomachache or fatigue, feelings of rejection or loss. The pain leads to arousal, a strong drive for discharge and stress reduction.

The second step in the production of anger occurs when people use *trigger thoughts*. These are attributions that blame and condemn others for the painful experience. Individuals use trigger thoughts to ignite feelings of anger and discharge some of their arousal. So, pain, stress, and arousal lead to blaming trigger thoughts, which lead to anger and more trigger thoughts and more anger in an escalating spiral. Thoughts and angry feelings become a feedback loop that can be self-perpetuating. It is often the feedback loop that keeps anger escalating for hours or even days without letup. It isn't possible to get angry without the presence of both painful arousal and trigger thoughts. That's why you will be taught to control both stress and blaming cognitions.

Ventilation Doesn't Work

Psychotherapists sometimes encourage their clients to get in touch with their anger. The theory behind this is that ventilation of anger is helpful. But anger is now better understood. New research shows that ventilation can make you angrier, because you rehearse all the bad and nasty things that others have done to you. It solidifies, or "freezes," your beliefs about another's wrongness and your sense of being victimized. Ventilation can not only serve to prolong anger; it can also make it easier to get angry in the future (it doesn't take much to remind you of what a jerk the other guy really is).

Anger Is Different From Aggression

Anger is an emotion. It's what happens when pain (feeling hurt), stress, or arousal and blaming trigger thoughts, combine to *create* feelings of anger. Aggression is *behavior.* It's something you do; it's a way of interacting with other people. Aggression can be in the form of either physical or verbal assault. You can be angry without being aggressive, and vice versa. Hit men are rarely angry when they pull the trigger; conversely, many angry people choose not to assault the target of their wrath.

Coping is Better Than Blaming

Every painful or hurtful situation presents a choice. You can blame somebody for what happened or you can use cognitive and relaxation coping skills to reduce your feelings of being upset, and then assert your needs in a nonblaming way. If you tell a roommate that she is lazy for not doing her chores, it really feels good for a minute to get it off your chest. But things will likely escalate from there. You both may end up shouting and your relationship may descend into the deep freeze. In a few weeks, it will be possible to make another choice. You might decide to use some relaxation skills to lower your stress level, change some of your trigger thoughts, and talk to your roommate, for example, nonblamingly about the problem of the chores. Very soon that will be a choice you can make.

Homework

- Continue self-monitoring in the anger log.

- Select two low-anger (rated three to four on a ten-point scale) scenes to work with during the next week.

SESSION THREE

The Shame Problem

Review: Survival Strategies for Shame

Surviving Shame

Progressive Muscle Relaxation

Relaxation Without Tension

Special Place Visualization

Breathing-Cued Relaxation

Cue-Controlled Relaxation

Combined Relaxation

Cognitive Control/Relaxation Training

Homework

The Problem with Shame

Review: Survival Strategies for Shame

A two-year old child explores the world. He finds a special place in the garden where he digs happily in the soft soil. He feels proud of his accomplishments. "Look at me," he wants to tell the world. "Look at what I can do. I am good."

"Just look at you!" shouts his mother. "Look at this mess. You are dirty. Your clothes are ruined. I'm very disappointed with you. You ought to be ashamed of yourself."

The child feels very small. He drops his head and stares at the ground. He sees his dirty hands and clothes and begins to feel dirty inside. He thinks there must be something very bad about him, something so bad he will never really be clean. He hears his mother's disdain. He feels defective.

Shame is not that you have done something wrong. Shame is that you <u>are</u> something wrong. The little boy above internalized the judgement of his mother. The mother's words came precisely at the developmental stage when a child is just beginning to assert some independence. Two years old is the time when children first begin to become a unique self, to say 'no', "I'm not you...I'm me". If the mother has some problem with her child's attempt toward autonomy, the child is ripe for experiencing excessive shame.

<u>Thoughts excessively shamed people defend against:</u>
- I am defective (damaged, broken, a mistake, flawed)
- I am dirty (soiled, ugly, unclean, impure, filthy, disgusting)
- I am incompetent (not good enough, inept, ineffectual)
- I am useless (worthless)
- I am unwanted (unloved, unappreciated, uncherished)
- I deserve to be abandoned (forgotten, unloved, left out)
- I am weak (impotent, feeble)
- I am bad (awful, dreadful, evil, despicable)
- I am nothing (worthless, invisible, unnoticed, empty)

Defenses against shame may, as it has been stated, help the person deal with their self worth problems temporarily, but in the long run it does not heal shame. No one can learn to benefit from shame by ignoring it.

Defenses against shame are survival strategies only; excessively shamed individuals must *learn* and *experience* that they are valuable persons who are worthy of love and respect.

Perfectionism

Another defense against shame is perfectionism. The perfectionist dreads making mistakes, because he thinks mistakes prove something is fundamentally wrong with him as a person. If he fails at something, he believes he is a total failure.

The perfectionist who is defending against shame seems only to recognize two states of being: perfect or shameful (all or nothing). This person fights desperately against being human because he equates accepting humanness with being a failure. But we are all simply human – people who must do the best we can given our limitations in strength, intelligence, creativity, and wisdom. It is not shameful to be less than perfect when none of us has a choice in the matter.

The perfectionist may not be particularly arrogant. He is not really trying to play God when he tries to be faultless. He is simply trying to hold shame at bay a little longer. He feels a tremendous pressure to perform, to demonstrate to the world and to himself that he is adequate. Constantly aware of the possibility of shame, he is convinced that others are watching for imperfections, and when they see his flaws, they will judge him to be worthless.

As you can see, the perfectionist is in a no-win situation. No matter how competent he is, regardless of how well he performs, despite all his successes, the perfectionist never feels more than one step ahead of shame. He can delay humiliation for a while, perhaps by working harder or longer than anyone else. But he cannot feel comfortable for very long either, because he does not know how to accept himself as a good, but limited, human being.

Ordinarily, shamed persons believe they are smaller or lower than others. The words *beneath contempt* describe how shame feels. But what if a shame based individual could convince himself that the opposite was true – that he really stood head and shoulders above everybody else? He would have discovered arrogance.

Can you think of anyone who uses perfectionism as a defense?
Is there a part of you that can use this defense?
How did you learn it?   (Use space on pg. 30 to write answers)

Rage

What happens when a person who is deeply shamed cannot withdraw from a threatening situation? Rage, another survival strategy against shame, is a likely response. The rageful person is shouting a warning: *Don't get any closer! You are getting too near my shame, and I won't let anyone see that part of me. Stay away or I will attack.* A rageful person is desperate to keep others far enough away so they cannot destroy him.

People are most apt to fly into a rage when they are surprised by a sudden attack on their identity. For example, a friend might offhandedly tell his buddy that his clothes are too cheap and loud for him to get a date with a certain woman. He might be joking, not intending to hurt his friend. But his friend is hurt. "What do you mean, I couldn't get a date with her? I sure look a whole lot better than you do – at least I don't walk with a limp like you." This shamed individual can only think to defend himself by cruelly attacking the other person.

Rage works. It drives people away and so protects the person from revealing his shame. Sometimes it works too well. People start to avoid rageful people who are oversensitive to supposed insults. "I would like to be John's friend," the person might say, "but whenever we start to get close, he finds something to get mad about. Then he attacks me for no reason."

The rageful person's strategy to defend against overwhelming shame is very debilitating to the person's self-esteem. This person will probably feel all the more defective when others become too scared to reach out to him. Rage breaks the connection between people and so increases the shamed person's shame. Chronically rageful people become trapped in a lonely world of their own making.

Anyone might respond with rage occasionally, especially when they are suddenly and unexpectedly embarrassed. But persons with excessive shame may express their anger more often. Their regular bouts of rage cover up deeper shame. Their attacks on others direct attention away from their sense of inadequacy.

Can you think of anyone who uses rage as a defense?
Is there a part of you that can use this defense?
How did you learn it?

Progressive Muscle Relaxation

Learning to relax can calm people down sufficiently in a provocative situation so that they can manage to think of better ways to handle the conflict. Complete the following exercise.

Make a fist with each hand and squeeze tight. Really concentrate on the feeling of tension in your fists and forearms. Hold for several seconds. Now relax. Feel the difference in your muscles. Notice a heaviness or warmth or tingling or whatever relaxation feels like for you. Now raise your arms and tighten them flexing your biceps. Hold the tension for seven seconds, and then let your arms fall limp by your sides. Once again notice feelings of relaxation, warmth or heaviness spreading through your arms as you let them drop. Really notice the contrast between tension and relaxation in your arms.

Now turn your attention to your upper face. Frown, squint your eyes shut as hard as you can, hold for seven seconds. Relax, and notice what it feels like to let go of tension in your upper face. Now tighten your jaw (not so hard that you'll crack a tooth) and push your tongue up against the roof of your mouth. Hold it for seven seconds. And relax. Notice what it feels like for your jaw to let go and be really loose. Now tense your neck muscles by shrugging your shoulders upward as far as you can (but don't try to pull your neck in like a turkey.) Wait a moment and relax. Let the relaxation move from your shoulders and neck up to your jaw and all the way to your forehead.

Now move your awareness to your chest and back. Take a deep breath and hold it. Tense your chest, shoulders, and upper back muscles, making your entire upper torso rigid. Take another deep breath. After seven seconds, let out the breath with a long, loud sigh, and let your torso go limp. Really melt down into the chair and focus on the difference between the tense and the relaxed states.

Now move your attention downward - into your stomach, lower back, and pelvic regions. Tighten your stomach, lower back and buttocks carefully. After seven seconds, relax and melt again into the chair. Notice feelings of warmth or heaviness spreading throughout your abdomen.

Now work on your legs. With your toes pointed straight out, like a ballerina, tense your thighs, your calves, and your feet. Hold this for seven seconds, then let your legs totally relax. Feel the heaviness and warmth flood into your legs as they go limp. Now tense your legs again, this time, pulling your toes up toward your head. Hold for seven seconds and let the relaxation spread like a wave throughout your entire body, into your abdomen and your chest, into your arms, your neck, your face and forehead, until you feel totally relaxed. Take another deep breath.

Relaxation Without Tension

Relaxation without tension can be substituted for progressive muscle relaxation when you wish to use a quicker less obvious technique. It can be used anywhere, without the potentially embarrassing ritual of progressive muscle relaxation.

Now go through the major muscle groups of your body in exactly the same sequence as the above progressive muscle relaxation. But this time don't tighten anything. Instead, scan each muscle group for tension and *relax away* any tightness you may experience. The catch phrase *Notice and relax* should be used frequently throughout this exercise. Be sure to begin and end the *relaxation without tension* exercise with a deep breath.

Go ahead and do the following exercise:

Take a deep breath. Focus on your arms and notice any tension you may feel there. Now relax away the tension. Just let it go. Notice and relax the tension. Feel the difference as you relax your arms. Now turn your attention to your upper face. Notice any tension and relax it away let it go. Notice and relax the tension. As you relax, really feel the difference in your upper face. Notice any tension in your jaw, and relax. Relax it away. Notice what it feels like for your jaw to let go, to be really loose.

Special Place Visualization

You will now identify your own special relaxation image. Make sure that all your major senses are involved. You should be able to see the shapes and colors, hear the sounds, feel the temperature and textures of the special place. If there are smells and tastes, include these also. Work carefully on constructing the image, developing as much detail as possible. Make sure that the image is capable of eliciting the emotion of contentment, safety, and calmness. Follow the following exercise:

Think about a place where you've felt especially safe, relaxed, or content. It could be the beach, mountains, meadows, your childhood bedroom, or a remembered moment of deep relaxation and peace. It can be a real place, or you could just make one up. Close your eyes and try to see the shapes and colors of your place. . Hear the sounds of your place; hear birds, or waves or babbling water. Feel the temperature of your place - is it cool or warm? Feel the textures of whatever you touch in your special place.

Make sure that everything in your special place makes you feel relaxed and safe. Change anything that doesn't feel right. If you want to add some trees, put them in. If you want the sound of a waterfall, add it. If you want to be alone, take the people out of your scene. If you want your dog, put him in.

Now use your special place visualization quickly, almost like a reflex, when things get stressful. Go ahead and visualize your special place, construct the scene as quickly as you can, really get into it until you feel the peacefulness, the safety, the relaxation. [Pause one minute.] Now get ready to leave the scene. Open your eyes, look around. Notice the environment. [Pause.] Now close your eyes again and return to your special place. See it, hear it, feel it, let it surround you and touch each of your senses. [Pause one minute.] Now, come back to the room and take a quick look at the environment again. [Pause.] One last time go back to the special place. Get there as quickly as you can, let it bathe your senses, see its shapes and colors, hear the sounds, feel it in your skin. [Pause one minute.] Now come back to the room. You can go to your special place any time you need to relax, to get out of a situation that provokes or disturbs you.

Breathing-Cued Relaxation

Start by putting one hand over your chest and the other over your abdomen, just above your belt line. Try taking a deep breath, way down into your belly. Really try to push your diaphragm down. As you breathe in, the hand on your abdomen should rise, while the hand on your chest remains relatively still. Focus all your attention on your belly - send your breath down, down, down to fill your belly. Let your breath slightly stretch, and relax your abdomen.

Cue-Controlled Relaxation

This deep-breathing technique stretches the diaphragm and very quickly relaxes abdominal tension associated with anger. It's crucial that you succeed in pushing the belly out with each intake or breath. Now it's time to select a word that will cue deep relaxation each time you repeat it. The word could be *relax* or *Om* or *one.* It might be a color, such as *green,* or a feeling, such as *love.* One- or two-syllable words are best.

With your cue word in mind, turn your attention again to your breathing. With each exhalation, say your cue word to yourself. Keep saying your cue word for the next ten breaths.

Combined Relaxation

Go through the entire progressive muscle relaxation procedure from session 1. At the end of this return to your special place imagery. After one minute, come back into the room and take a series of three deep, abdominal breaths. Make sure that the abdominal hand is rising, while the chest hand remains relatively still. Then, for the next ten breaths repeat your cue word for relaxation. Remind yourself to say your special word with each exhalation.

Cognitive Control/Relaxation Training

It's now time to combine cognitive and stress-reduction techniques. The best way to achieve this is through the use of imagery.

Coping Skill Rehearsal

Select two anger scenes from your Anger Log in the three-to-four range. Read the following example before you begin the rehearsal of your two scenes:

Therapist: Jill, what's your anger scene?

Client: John's late picking up the kids again and the playschool people called. He's always late, it really ticks me off.

Therapist: Okay, what kind of trigger thoughts did you use?

Client: I guess I'm saying he *should* be there. Also, I'm magnifying a bit - he's not *always* late.

Therapist: How could you cope with the trigger thought? What could you say to yourself that would cool the anger?

Client: I guess I could remind myself that he's only late once in a while, and it's usually because he's harried.

Therapist: Anything else that would help from the coping statements?

Client: He does the best he can.

Therapist: Does that really help - do you believe that at all?

Client: Not really.

Therapist: How about a more general coping statement that just reminds you to calm down, or that anger doesn't help?

Client: Yeah. "There's nothing gained in getting mad." That's true. I just get crazy for nothing.

It's time to begin *coping skill rehearsal.* Here's what you do.

1. Go through the complete relaxation sequence: progressive muscle relaxation, relaxation without tension, special place visualization, breathing-cued relaxation, and cue-controlled relaxation.
2. Now visualize one of the anger scenes. Get involved in the scene as if it were really happening. Use your trigger thoughts and notice any feelings of arousal.

When you have experienced anger for approximately 30 seconds, erase the scene and return to some of your relaxation coping skills. But during those 30 seconds really try to be there. Notice the setting, the details, the colors, and the shapes. Notice any sounds. Notice your physical sensations in the scene. Try to make it real. Remember your trigger thoughts - really let yourself go. Get into the blames or the shoulds. Tell yourself you're entitled to better treatment, or they're being unfair. Tell yourself they're doing it to you. Label it bad or stupid or selfish. As your anger builds, notice what it feels like inside your body. Notice the arousal and growing tension. Where in your body does the tension grow first? As you notice the tension, try to let yourself get even angrier. Keep fanning the flames. What's the matter with them, anyway? Why do they keep doing this to you? Angrier. Angrier and angrier. Really feeling it in your body. Tell yourself how outrageous, how wrong, and how unfair. Feel more and more anger.

3. Use several of the coping thoughts that might be helpful in the situation.

Repeat the entire sequence, using the second anger scene.

Are there coping statements you can develop that would change this into a problem or a hassle, but not an overwhelming nightmare? What could you say to yourself that would demagnify your feelings in this situation?

Here are some helpful coping statements:

- Everyone makes the best choice possible.
- I can stay calm and relaxed.
- No one is right, no one is wrong. We just have different needs.
- Getting upset won't help.
- There's nothing to be gained in getting mad.
- I'm free to want things, but others are also free to say no.

Continue to repeat the relaxation/anger scene/relaxation sequence two to six times. After the first two sequences use relaxation without tension instead of progressive muscle relaxation. It saves time. Following each sequence write down your coping thoughts and think about which ones are working and not working in a particular anger scene. Modify your coping thoughts or develop new ones if you' re having difficulty developing coping thoughts that help, go back to the trigger thoughts and get a clear sense of what you are saying to ignite anger. Explore how the trigger thought may be unrealistic in the situation and develop a more realistic appraisal of what is likely to be going on.

Homework
- Practice the complete relaxation sequence of progressive muscle relaxation (or relaxation without tension), special place visualization, breathing-cued relaxation, and cue-controlled relaxation daily for the next week. Mark a *p* on the practice log for each day of relaxation practice completed.

- Practice relaxation without tension daily, as well as other relaxation techniques. Mark a *p* in the anger log for each day of completed practice.

- Now in the anger log record your coping efforts under each anger situation. Note whether emotional arousal and/or aggressive scores decreased after coping procedures.

- Select two more anger scenes, this time in the five-to-six range, for use in the next session.

SESSION FOUR

The Shame Problem

Chronic Shame is Relentless and Devastating

Surviving Shame

More Coping Skills Rehearsal

ABC Cognitive Theory

Trigger Thoughts

Entitlement

Fairness

Global labeling

Coping Statements

For Trigger Thoughts

General Coping Thoughts and Strategies

Homework

40

The Problem with Shame

Review: **Survival Strategies for Shame**

A middle-aged man has almost no identity of his own. He tries to please everyone he meets, to become whatever they want him to be. He wears a mask of pleasantness so well that even he has no idea what would happen if he took it off. He thinks that if people were to see through his mask, they would discover that he is worthless or disgusting. They might not ever want to speak with him again.

Chronic shame is relentless and devastating. The recovery process requires shattering the myth that you must live with constant shame. We call this situation a myth because nobody has to live forever in shame. There is room enough for everyone in this world. There is no such thing as a subhuman. The wonderful thing about shame, even excessive shame, is that people can learn to live with it and grow spiritually richer in the process. But the person who is deeply shamed must learn how to challenge his belief that he is intrinsically valueless. Excessively shamed persons become accustomed to interpreting events from the perspective of disgrace. They need to discover how to see the world from a less threatening perspective. They need to challenge and discard their own myth that dooms them to a life of feeling shame. For instance, the man mentioned above will need to begin to accept his positive characteristics and find the courage to take off his mask so that he can discover his true self.

- Stop being Critical of Yourself
- Stop Comparing Yourself
- Change Relationships that Confirm Your Shame

As stated several times defenses against shame may help the person deal with self worth problems temporarily, but in the long run they do not heal shame. No one can learn to benefit from shame by ignoring it. Defenses against shame are survival strategies only; excessively shamed individuals must *learn* and *experience* that they are valuable persons who are worthy of love and respect. The way out of shame is to come out of hiding.

Arrogance

Another defense against shame is when a person convinces himself that he is better than everyone else is. There are two ways of displaying arrogance: grandiosity or contempt. Grandiosity is when a person inflates his sense of self-worth so that he believes he is better than others are. Contempt is when a person puts down someone else to make that person seem smaller than herself.

For example, imagine two people as two equally inflated balloons. Now imagine pumping up one of the balloons until it is so full of hot air that it is ready to burst. That is grandiosity. The grandiose person hides his shame from himself and others by filling up with pretentiousness and false pride. He needs to feel superior to cover up his basic sense of shame. He deludes himself into thinking that he is naturally the best of all living creatures.

Now imagine deflating the other balloon. That is contempt. The contemptuous person will find a way to deflate other people, making them feel weak, incompetent, and shameful. This person defends against shame by giving it away to someone else. He feels better about himself only when he reduces others to nothing.

Some excessively shamed persons practice grandiosity; others practice contempt. Many use both forms of arrogance to protect themselves against their inner sense of shame. An arrogant person places himself on a pedestal where nobody can see his shame, not even himself. The price he pays is not being connected to others. The beauty of intimacy with others cannot warm someone on a pedestal. The arrogant person has set himself apart from all those who would or could love him. True, he avoids feeling worse than others do by exchanging feelings of inferiority for feelings of superiority. But he fails to touch the center of his pain – his shame.

Can you think of anyone who uses arrogance as a defense? Is there a part of you that can use this defense? How did you learn it?

Exhibitionism

The last survival strategy is exhibitionism. This seems to be a paradox because the person, who is shamed, instead of hiding, calls attention to herself. *Go ahead; look at me if you want,* the exhibitionist seems to say. *I've got nothing to hide.* This person may act outrageously, flaunting his sexuality, dress, or behavior.

The exhibitionist displays what he would really like to hide. For example, many persons who were victims of sexual abuse as children suffer deep shame as adults. Some of them, however, discover they feel a little more control and a little less pain by wearing extremely seductive clothing or by engaging in numerous sexual encounters. They have survived their early shame experiences by converting their embarrassment and humiliation into public flamboyance.

Exhibitionism is a particularly harmful defense against shame. Every time the exhibitionist goes on display she sets herself further apart from people who are offended or shocked by her behavior. Threat only increases her shame, which she suppresses by showing off all the more. The exhibitionist eventually becomes isolated, alone, the object of scorn or pity, and once again, ashamed.

Can you think of anyone who uses exhibitionism as a defense? Is there a part of you that can use this defense? How did you learn it?

More Coping Skills Rehearsal

Repeat the *coping skill rehearsal* from last session.

1. Go through the complete relaxation sequence: progressive muscle relaxation, relaxation without tension, special place visualization, breathing-cued relaxation, and cue-controlled relaxation.

2. Now visualize one of the anger scenes from the 5 to 6 range. Get involved in the scene as if it were really happening. Use your trigger thoughts and notice any feelings of arousal. When you have experienced anger for approximately 30 seconds (as done previously), erase the scene and return to some of your relaxation coping skills. But during those 30 seconds really try to be there. Notice the setting, the details, the colors, and the shapes. Notice any sounds. Notice your physical sensations in the scene. Try to make it real. Remember your trigger thoughts - really let yourself go. Get into the blames or the shoulds. Tell yourself you're entitled to better treatment, or they're being unfair. Tell yourself they're doing it to you. Label it bad or stupid or selfish. As your anger builds, notice what it feels like inside your body. Notice the arousal and growing tension. Where in your body does the tension grow first? As you notice the tension, try to let yourself get even angrier. Keep fanning the flames. What's the matter with them, anyway? Why do they keep doing this to you? Angrier. Angrier and angrier. Really feeling it in your body. Tell yourself how outrageous, how wrong, and how unfair. Feel more and more anger.

3. Use several of the coping thoughts that might be helpful in the situation. Repeat the entire sequence, using the second anger scene.

   Are their coping statements you can develop that would change this into a problem or a hassle, but not an overwhelming nightmare? What could you say to yourself that would demagnify your feelings in this situation?

   Review these helpful coping statements:

   - Everyone makes the best choice possible.
   - I can stay calm and relaxed.
   - No one is right, no one is wrong. We just have different needs.
   - Getting upset won't help.

- There's nothing to be gained in getting mad.
- I'm free to want things, but others are also free to say no.

Continue to repeat the relaxation/anger scene/relaxation sequence two to six times. After the first two sequences use relaxation without tension instead of progressive muscle relaxation. It saves time. Following each sequence write down your coping thoughts and think about which ones are working and not working in a particular anger scene. Modify your coping thoughts or develop new ones if you' re having difficulty developing coping thoughts that help, go back to the trigger thoughts and get a clear sense of what you are saying to ignite anger. Explore how the trigger thought may be unrealistic in the situation and develop a more realistic appraisal of what is likely to be going on.

ABC Cognitive Theory

This is the opportunity for you to put all the relaxation skills together into one sequence. It should be practiced at home to the point where it is over learned and automatic. Follow this exercise:

Imagine that you're working in an office where several co-workers play radios at their desks. The sound is low, but you nevertheless find it distracting. Really visualize the scene for a moment. Now imagine that you are saying to yourself how inconsiderate they are, how selfish, how uncaring of the needs of others. Imagine yourself thinking that they're doing this to you because they simply don't give a damn about anyone but themselves. Do you notice your feelings?

Now let's imagine something else. You're in the same office; the same co-workers are playing their radios. But instead, you say to yourself: 'I can't think, I can't concentrate, and I'm never going to get my work done. I'm never going to get this in on time. I'm not going to be able to function here. How can I keep my job if I can't do a simple task like this when there's a little noise?' What feelings come up now? Look for and reinforce any

45

responses that have to do with anxiety. Now let's go back to the same situation once more. The radios are playing and you think to yourself, 'I never fit in anywhere, things always bother me, and my colleagues will probably be resentful if I ask them to turn their radios down. I'm so rattlebrained that I can't even think with a little music in the background. I can't handle the slightest stress or problem.' What do you feel now?

Dr. Albert Ellis developed what is called the ABC model of emotion, where *A* (event) leads to *B* (thought, interpretation, assumption, and appraisal), which in turn leads to *C* (emotion). When you get angry, it feels as though the event is making you angry. It feels as though somebody is doing something to you and the only natural response is anger. What really happens is that the event starts you thinking. Like the person in the office, you can think different kinds of thoughts. You can think about dangerous or catastrophic consequences and get anxious, or you can think about your failures and inadequacies and get depressed. Or you can think blaming thoughts and label others as bad or selfish or stupid. Then you get angry.

The same situation will produce different emotions, depending on what you think about it. That's where the trigger thoughts come in. You can't really get angry until you respond to the situation with trigger thoughts that get you hot. Right now, we have an opportunity to learn some thoughts that will cool down the anger response. These are thoughts that take away the sting of blame and help you look at things with a little more detachment.

Imagine you were in that office with the radios and you said to yourself, 'This is no big deal. They're having a good time. They don't know they're bugging me. I'll find a diplomatic way to get them to turn the radios down.' Notice that these are cooling thoughts. The anger melts away as you stop blaming. You begin to feel that there's something you can do about it.

Trigger Thoughts

Take a look again at the Coping Statements describing the major trigger thoughts. Now read the following:

Shoulds

Anger is often heard as a judgment based on a set of rules about how people should and should not act. People who behave according to the rules are right, and those who break the rules are wrong. Angry people think that others know and accept their rules but deliberately choose to violate them. The first problem with shoulds, however, is that people with whom you feel angry rarely agree with you.

Their perception of the situation leaves them blameless and justified. Other people's rules always seem to exempt them from the judgments you think they deserve. The second problem with shoulds is that people *never* do what they should do. They only do what is reinforcing and rewarding for them to do. It turns out that shoulds are one person's values and needs imposed on someone else who has very different values and needs. Below are some coping responses to shoulds.

1. What needs influence him or her to act this way?

2. What problems, fears, or limitations influence this behavior?

3. What beliefs or values influence him or her to act this way?

4. Forget the shoulds, they only get me upset.

5. People do what *they* want to do, not what *I* think they should do.

There are three special types of shoulds that are particularly upsetting. Let me describe, first of all, the entitlement fallacy.

Entitlement

The entitlement fallacy is based on the simple belief that because you want something very much, you ought to have it. The felt intensity of the perceived need justifies the demand that someone else provide for it. The underlying feeling is that you are entitled to certain things in life, and if you don't get them, someone is deliberately, selfishly or maliciously depriving you.

The problem with entitlement is that a person confuses desire with obligation. It feels as though wanting something very much somehow makes it unacceptable for others to say no. But entitlement can be very damaging to relationships. It requires that the other person give up his or her limits and boundaries for you. It says that your need and your pain must come first. Some relevant coping statements are listed below:

1. I am free to want, but he or she is free to say no.

2. I have my limits and you have your limits.

3. I have the right to say no, and so do you.

4. My desire doesn't obligate you to meet it.

Fairness

The fallacy of fairness rests on the idea that there is some absolute standard of correct and fair behavior which people should understand and live up to. When you believe that the concept of fairness applies to relationships, you end up keeping an emotional ledger book that balances what you give against what you get in a relationship. The problem is that no two people agree on what fairness is, and in personal relationships, there is no court or arbiter to help them. What's fair becomes a totally subjective judgment, depending entirely on what each person expects, needs, or hopes for from the other. Since the standard of fairness is inevitably a measure of one's own beliefs and wants, people can literally call anything fair or unfair. Calling someone unfair just inflames the argument. It never convinces anyone or solves a conflict. You can use the following statements:

1. Our needs are equally important.

2. Each need is legitimate - we can negotiate.

Escalation occurs through the use of exaggeration words like *terrible, awful, disgusting* or *horrendous.* You may over generalize by using words such as *always, all, every, never.* He's always as slow as molasses. She's awful with the whole support staff. He never helps. This is going to be a horrible mess next week. These magnifications tend to crank up your sense of anxiety and sense of victimization. When you exaggerate the problem, you start to feel really deeply wronged. They're bad and you're innocent. You can use these coping statements:

1. No more *always* or *never.*
2. Let the facts speak for themselves.
3. Accuracy, not exaggeration.

Global labeling

Global labeling is the act of making sweeping negative judgments. You label people as bad, stupid, selfish, assholes, screw-ups, and so on. Global labels fuel your anger by turning the other person into someone who is totally bad and worthless. Instead of focusing on a particular behavior, you indict the entire person. You inflate one aspect of the person to fill the entire picture of who he or she is. Once you've made someone totally despicable, it's very easy to get angry. You can use these coping statements:

1. No one's bad - people do the best they can.
2. No mean labels.
3. Be specific.

Coping Statements for Trigger Thoughts

- Forget shoulds - they only upset me.
- People do what *they* want to do, not what *I* think they should do. I am free to want, but they are free to say no.
- I have the right to say no, and so do they.
- My desire doesn't obligate them to fulfill it. Our needs are equally important.
- Each need is legitimate - we can negotiate.
- We change only when change is reinforced and they are capable of changing.
- People only change when they want to.
- I may not like it, but they're doing the best they can.
- I'm not helpless - I can take care of myself in this situation.
- Don't second-guess the motives of others.
- Assume nothing; or else check out every assumption.
- No more *always* or *never.*
- Accuracy, not exaggeration.
- No one's bad, people do the best they can.
- No mean labels.

General Coping Thoughts and Strategies

- Take a deep breath and relax.
- Getting upset won't help.
- Just as long as I keep my cool, I'm in control.
- Easy does it - there's nothing to be gained in getting mad.
- I'm not going to let him get to me.
- I can't change her with anger; I'll just upset myself.
- I can find a way to say what I want to without anger.
- Stay calm - no sarcasm, no attacks.
- I can stay calm and relaxed.
- No one is right, no one is wrong. We just have different needs.
- Stay cool, make no judgments.
- No matter what is said, I know I'm a good person.
- I'll stay rational - anger won't solve anything.
- I don't like it, but he's using the best problem-solving strategy available to him right now.
- Her opinion isn't important I won't be pushed to losing control.

Homework

- Go through the Coping Statement and mark the responses that seem most useful to you.
- Continue relaxation practice.
- Continue the anger log, with particular attention on the coping process in each anger situation. Make sure that you rate any changes in emotional arousal and aggression following your coping response.
- Generate two anger scenes in the seven-to-eight range that will be used during the next session.

SESSION FIVE

The Shame Problem

Significant Problems Associated with Shame

Shame and the Self Centered Universe

Shame and the Fear of Abandonment

"I Will Be Whatever You Want Me to Be"

Self Sabotage

Self Abuse

Self Neglect

The Tendency to Humiliate Others

Compulsive/Addictive Behaviors

More Coping Skills Rehearsal

Coping Skills Rehearsal – Coping in the Scene

Homework

The Shame Problem

Significant Problems Associated with Shame

A forty-year old man has completely taken over a small party. He talks loudly and endlessly about his life, insisting that everyone listen to his stories. When someone tries to change the topic, he ignores him or her. He insists on staying center stage, as if he thinks the rest of the world exists only to tell him how wonderful he is. He seems completely full of himself and empty of others.

There are some significant problems associated with shame. You can start to help yourself by noticing how excessive shame contributes to these problems.

Shame and the Self Centered Universe

Most people learn when they are young that they cannot be the center of the universe. Some people do not want to accept this idea. Perhaps they never learned to gracefully relinquish being the center of attention when they were children. This situation begins to become shame deficiency, shamelessness. The person wants to be placed on a pedestal where they can be adored. They are egotistical to the point of having no room to care about others. This is different from arrogance where the person consciously behaves in a way to compensate for a felt inadequacy. The shameless person has a distorted belief system leading to shame deficiency.

Shame and the Fear of Abandonment

The fear of abandonment is central in people who have excessive shame. Abandonment seems quite possible to people who believe that they are basically worthless and unlovable. Why would anyone stay with her when there are so many better persons in the world? Excessive shame prevents people from believing that they are good enough to be cherished.

"I Will Be Whatever You Want Me to Be"

Fearing abandonment, people who are shamed may try to please others by becoming whoever others want them to be. Their reasoning is clear: *I'm certain that they would be revolted if they saw the real me. I must please them by being a person they would be proud of. That's the only way they will keep me.*

People spend most of their time reacting to others. Their self-worth depends on the praise and criticism they receive from outside themselves.

Self Sabotage

Self-sabotage is a way to be self-destructive. A person sabotages herself when she "forgets" to enroll on time in a program that would enhance her career, or consciously refuses to take medication as prescribed that would ease her depression. She undermines her chances for success and happiness because she thinks she does not deserve anything positive. Internalized shame demands failure. This person chooses continuing shame over success at least in part because her rage at herself allows no room for competence or achievement.

Self Abuse

Self-abuse is an active result of shame. Here, the person who is deeply shamed seeks out ways to damage herself. Certainly, some shame-connected addictive behaviors are nothing less than slow suicide – the alcoholic who continues to drink despite liver damage for example. Other forms of self-abuse include calling oneself names and knowingly entering into damaging relationships with shamers.

Self Neglect

Self-neglect occurs when a person who is excessively shamed ignores her own needs by, for example, failing to see a physician despite a severe illness, refusing to eat balanced meals, and neglecting her appearance. Each of these actions demonstrates passive self-hatred.

The Tendency to Humiliate Others

Shame is a threat to a person's basic sense of being. The excessively shamed person feels small, weak, vulnerable, and exposed. She may rage against herself because she feels unacceptable. She might also find this self-hatred unendurable. Sometimes, in order to survive, a person who is excessively shamed transfers her hatred on to others, treating them with the disdain and contempt they often experienced themselves. Unfortunately excessively shamed people become parents who attack and humiliate those who they have the most power over – their family. The family victims receive the parents' criticism, verbal and sometimes physical assaults, never allowing for any success or happiness. The more the parent loves them, the more he/she needs to reduce them to nothing so they cannot do the same to him/her. The parent shames to avoid his or her own shame.

Compulsive/Addictive Behaviors

Shame and addiction are natural partners. The more chronically and excessively shamed a person is, the more likely he will be attracted to anything that promises relief from internal pain and emptiness. The answer must lie outside himself in the "magic" of alcohol, other drugs, mystical religious movements, consumer goods, sex, food, work, the latest therapy, fad, etc. He is trying to fill the void that has been at least partially created by excessive shame. He simply cannot stand being in pain or feeling empty inside. Note here that shame alone, does not cause addiction any more than an addiction causes shame. Each contributes to the other. The person who is excessively shamed is a high-risk candidate to become addicted, while the addicted person frequently becomes more and more shamed as the addiction worsens.

More Coping Skills Rehearsal

Coping Skills Rehearsal – Coping in the Scene

Identify the two anger scenes that you'll use in the seven-to-eight range. This week, the coping skills rehearsal will have a slightly different structure. From now on you will not leave the anger scene 30 seconds after you have experienced arousal. Instead, you'll remain in the scene and practice your relaxation and cognitive coping skills *while the anger scene continues.* Follow this exercise:

Really get into the anger scene - remember your trigger thoughts, really try to feel the growing tension on a physical level. Remind yourself of the unfairness, the wrongness, and the outrageousness of the offense. When you really feel the anger, start your coping responses. Keep pushing, and pushing up the anger. But once you get there, once you're angry, start relaxing. Start breathing deeply. Recall your special place. Focus on your body; notice tension and relax it away. Talk back to the trigger thoughts. What can you say to cope? Try some coping statements and see which ones work. Do whatever works for you to cool down. Stay with it until you've found a way to control anger. When you've controlled your anger, terminate the scene. When you've relaxed away your anger, when you've talked back to your anger, when you've coped with your anger, terminate the scene.

Read the following example of George and his group therapist:

Therapist: How are you doing with the scene, George?

George: I get pissed off, but then I stay upset. The anger has a life of its own.

Therapist: What are your trigger thoughts?

George: That my girlfriend's selfish, that she doesn't care about me.

Therapist: What have you tried to say to yourself to cope?

George: That we each have different needs, that I shouldn't assume the worst about her.

Therapist: But that doesn't work?

George: Not a bit.

Therapist: Ideas from the group?

Al: How about just reminding yourself to stop judging her?

Sylvia: Focus on asking for what you want and assume you'll both have to compromise.

Mark: How 'bout just telling yourself to say what you want without anger?

Therapist: Any of that helpful?

George: I think just reminding myself to tell her what I want without anger.

Therapist: Are you remembering to take a deep breath?

George: I really didn't do that.

Therapist: That will help, too. What makes your girlfriend so adamant at times? Do you know?

George: She thinks I don't spend enough time with her.

Therapist: Does that mean she's afraid you don't care about her, too?

George: I guess that might be true.

Therapist: So you could say to yourself, "We're both scared here. I'd better deal with this without anger."

You are expected to keep working on your scenes until you have mastered the anger. As soon as you are sufficiently angry switch immediately into the coping mode. Once the scene is terminated, you should continue the cognitive and relaxation coping efforts until you start the next anger scene. Continue this process for up to six repetitions. Always alternate between the two anger scenes.

Homework

- Continue self-monitoring, paying particular attention to the coping efforts in each anger situation. Continue to rate emotional arousal and aggression *after* the coping efforts.
- Develop two high-anger scenes, in the nine-to-ten range, for use in the next Session.

SESSION SIX

The Shame Problem

Current Shaming Relationships

Still More Coping Skills Rehearsal

Coping in the Scene II

Homework

The Shame Problem

Current Shaming Relationships

"Sometimes I wonder if anybody in the whole world cares about me. Yes, I have a lot of people in my life. But they always want me to take care of them. When I have something I need help with or when I need to talk about my feelings, they all seem to vanish. I feel more like a servant than a friend."

"I call myself the most terrible names. Sometimes it's because I've made a mistake or said something dumb. Sometimes I haven't done anything bad at all that I can think of. I hear this voice inside screaming at me that I'm the most miserable excuse for a human being that ever walked on earth. The rest is unprintable. I feel loaded down with self-hatred."

Shame is corrosive. It eats away at a person's dignity, pride, and self-respect. Unfortunately, many people become embroiled in shaming relationships that feature daily episodes of humiliation. These relationships may be one-sided – only one member shames the other. One-way shame often occurs when one person enjoys a power advantage over the other. Two-way shaming relationships happen when both parties vigorously and regularly shame each other. These people engage in shaming contests in which the goal is to degrade the other more.

Shaming relationships are dehumanizing. *All of us deserve to be treated with respect, no matter what the nature of our association with another person is. Others deserve our respect.* Any relationship that centers on shame dishonors its participants.

Stop here for a moment and identify two relationships you are aware of which you believe are shaming relationships. Describe how the shaming occurs.

1.

2.

63

Excessive shame begins for the infant with his first significant relationship. This is usually the mother-child relationship because the mother is most often involved as the primary care-taking adult. The shaming continues to develop in the family of origin, and is encouraged by an overly shamed-focused culture. (The scope of this Workbook does not allow for thorough discussion of this development)

One present source of shame may exist in your relationships. Few persons are strong enough to stand up to continuous shame attacks by important people in their lives. Who will feel really good when told repeatedly that they are incompetent, worthless, ugly, or stupid? Who can feel healthy pride while listening to messages that he will never be good enough to satisfy their family, friends, or employer? The formula is simple: the more people are shamed by others, the more shameful they will feel. Every person is entitled to a life free from excessive shame. The more a person has suffered shame, the more he expects it.

It is easy to have strong feelings when thinking about shaming relationships. You may find yourself reacting strongly, especially if you are now in a shaming relationship. Keep a few thoughts in mind:

1. Someone who regularly shames you may be unaware that he/she is doing so (not all shame episodes are deliberate).
2. You may be both a victim and a victimizer. This means that persons who are shamed by others often also repeatedly spread shame as well.
3. Shaming relationships can be changed. If both parties in a relationship realize there is too much shame, they may be able to alter their behavior.

Answer the following questions:

Do you know anyone who is in a shaming relationship?

Have you ever been involved in a shaming relationship?

What might you reasonably do to begin to change a shaming relationship?

More Coping Skills Rehearsal

Coping in the Scene II

Identify the two anger scenes that you'll use in the seven-to-eight range. As in the last session, the coping skills rehearsal will have a slightly different structure.

Really get into the anger scene (as you have done previously) - remember your trigger thoughts, really try to feel the growing tension on a physical level. Remind yourself of the unfairness, the wrongness, and the outrageousness of the offense. When you really feel the anger, start your coping responses. Keep pushing; keep pushing up the anger. But once you get there, once you're angry, start relaxing. Start breathing deeply. Recall your special place. Focus on your body; notice tension and relax it away. Talk back to the trigger thoughts. What can you say to cope? Try some coping statements and see which ones work. Do whatever works for you to cool down. Your hand should stay up until you've found a way to control anger. When you've controlled your anger, terminate the scene. When you've relaxed away your anger, when you've talked back to your anger, when you've coped with your anger, terminate the scene.

You are expected to keep working on the scene until you have mastered the anger. As soon as you are sufficiently aroused switch immediately into the coping mode. Once the scene is terminated, you should continue the cognitive and relaxation coping efforts until the next anger scene is introduced. Continue this process for up to six repetitions. Always alternate between the two anger scenes.

Homework

- Continue monitoring anger and coping in the anger log.

- Memorize RCR active response #1

SESSION SEVEN

The Shame Problem

Shaming Yourself

Description of Response Choice Rehearsal

Response Choice Rehearsal

Active Responses

Passive Responses

First RCR Response: Ask for What You Want

Homework

The Shame Problem

Shaming Yourself

"I feel totally empty – worthless and useless. My life has lost its meaning. I set goals for myself that nobody could meet, and then I despair about my failures. No matter what I do, I can never be good enough to please myself. The funny thing is that I put all this pressure on myself. Nobody else is unhappy with me. Why can't I live with myself when everybody else can?"

All people occasionally shame themselves, in other words, they are self-critical. After all, shame is part of life, and moderate shame can help you grow emotionally mature. Excessively shamed persons, however, are so full of shame they regularly attack themselves with this weapon. These individuals can truly be called excessively shamed because they respond to the world through the lens of their shame. They suffer from such an excess of this feeling that they seem to take their shame lens wherever they go.

The excessively shamed person expects others to confirm his badness by putting him down with criticism and contempt. Still, even a positive response from others is often irrelevant to the excessively shamed person. The crucial point here is that this person is constantly telling himself that he is no good. He expects others to confirm his shamefulness mainly because <u>he</u> is convinced they will view him in the same way he sees himself. Nor will this person quickly change his self-perception in the face of praise and acceptance. He will stubbornly cling to the idea that there is something fundamentally wrong with him. He is ashamed to exist.

The excessively shamed person has taken his shame into the very center of his being. His shame comes automatically to him because it is a deeply engrained habit of thinking. The example at the top of this page of the person who constantly calls himself names illustrates this pattern. That person's core of self-hatred and disgust gets activated time after time. He ends up attacking himself mercilessly.

People lose energy when they give themselves these messages. Some give themselves so many of these messages they consistently withdraw from healthy relationships or healthy activities. They retreat or prepare to withdraw whenever they believe they are once again doing something wrong.

Excessively shamed individuals sometimes have perfectionistic traits even though, deep down, they are imperfectionists. The house must be spotless before company arrives; a project never gets finished because it has several flaws; a person, trying to do a job faultlessly, stays at work or school long after others have gone home. It seems that the excessively shamed person must take great pride in his accomplishments in one realm of life and none in other realms. Whatever the manifestation of the excessive shame, the goal is to avoid humiliation. His failures seem permanent to him – no matter what he does they cannot be redeemed. His successes seem temporary – they could vanish in an instant. Shame is never far away.

Shame that cannot be removed gradually turns into self-hatred. It is as if there is a "black hole" in the person's soul into which his goodness is lost forever, leaving a residue of disgust and contempt. Thinking only about the badness inside, he misses the beauty of his own humanity. He sees ugliness instead of beauty, shame instead of grace, and weakness instead of strength. Self-hatred is not subtle or sophisticated. The messages we are referring to are basic and crude. They may include profanity and deprecation.

List three messages that you struggle with the most:

1.

2.

3.

Across the page list the new statement you need to learn to make. For example:

Old Statement	New Statement
I am unlovable	I am lovable
I am weak	I am strong

Description of Response Choice Rehearsal *

Upon reviewing the description below,* go through each of the RCR responses. Not all six of the responses will be appropriate for a given anger situation. It is appropriate to switch from one response to another to cope with growing anger or escalation. Although a single anger control strategy often fails during provocations, the ability to use a variety of strategies and responses in succession increases the likelihood of resolution.

The key attitude to hold during angry situations is problem solving rather than vengeance. This is a slightly different version of the earlier "cope-don't-blame" concept. An avenger wants to punish and injure the offending party to the same degree that he or she has been hurt. Pain must be paid back. A problem solving attitude assumes that the problem is a matter of conflicting needs. There are no right or wrong about it; each person's needs are legitimate and important. The goal is to work toward agreement through discussion and compromise.

*Response Choice Rehearsal (McKay, Rogers, & McKay, 1989) is a method for handling conflict that has the advantage of requiring very little thought or preparation. You can do it when you're stressed and you don't have time to plan a response. You can still do it even when your buttons are pushed, you're getting angry, and you want to smash somebody. The bad news is that you'll have to memorize the six RCR responses. But the good news is that they really will work to de-escalate some of your conflicts *while making room for real problem solving.*

Response Choice Rehearsal *

Active Responses

1. *Ask for what you want:* I'm feeling {what's bothering me is}_____. And what I think I need{want/would like}in this situation is _____.

2. *Negotiate:* What would you propose to solve this problem?

3. *Self-Care:* If {the problem} goes on, I'll have to {your self-care solution} in order to take care of myself.

Passive Responses

4. *Get information:* What do you need in this situation? What concerns {worries} you in this situation? What's hurting {bothering} you in this situation?

5. *Acknowledge:* So what *you* want is _____. So what concerns {worries} you is _____. So what hurts {bothers}you is _____.

6. *Withdraw:* It feels like we're starting to get upset. I want to stop and cool off for a while.

*McKay, Rogers, & McKay, 1989

Once you have had an opportunity to examine the RCR description, read the following six points:

1. RCR consists of six pre-learned strategies for adaptively coping with angry encounters.

2. Strategies are divided into active and passive responses.

3. RCR will help you to cope even when you are extremely angry.

4. RCR will enable you to learn adaptive reactions that help solve problems rather than escalate tension.

5. RCR will keep you from getting stuck with a response that isn't working, and will make it more likely that you'll find a response that will get you what you want.

6. RCR will help you experience anger as a signal to cope and try a new response rather than as a signal to escalate your angry feelings.

When one RCR response doesn't work (because you're just too angry or things are still escalating), you simply choose another one. Eventually, you'll find a response that decreases tension and gives you enough emotional safety to start reaching for some kind of agreement.

You'll notice that there are active and passive responses. Either kind can be effective. But the key to understanding how to use RCR is to keep in mind that no single response is likely to be the right one, the answer. The first thing you try might not have much impact on your anger or on the anger of the provoking person. Your second response still might not work. Even your third may be a complete miss. But taken together, a series of adaptive responses is quite likely to cool you down and eventually deescalate the conflict. Sooner or later, you're going to find something that will turn the anger around, or at least get you out of the situation.

In RCR, you use your anger as a red flag that signals you to switch to a new coping response. So instead of fueling more aggression, your anger is a sign to change tack, to shift your strategies. Anger is merely an indication that you're stuck, the current response isn't working, or solving the problem. When you're proficient at RCR, anger will just mean, 'I'd better try something new.'

First RCR Response: Ask for What You Want

a) Memorize these opening lines:

"I'm feeling (what's bothering me is)

_____.

And what I think I need (or want or would like in this situation) is

_____.

Rules

a) What is bothering you (your feeling) is optional. Include this if you think it's important information that will help the other person to be more responsive. If the other person is an intimate, he or she deserves to know your reactions.

b) Ask for something behavioral, not attitudinal.

c) Ask for something specific, limited to one or two things.

d) Develop a fallback position – for instance, the minimum change that would be acceptable to you. This gives you room to negotiate.

Read the following *Role-Play* between George and his therapist:

George: (provocateur) This is ridiculous, rushing like this. So damn compulsive. For God's sake, relax!

Therapist: I'm feeling really anxious that we're going to be late for the surprise party. What I want is to be at least thirty minutes early.

George: (provocateur) Thirty minutes of just standing around waiting for things to start? Forget it! That's nuts!

Therapist: (fallback position): I'm feeling really anxious that we'll miss the surprise. Fifteen minutes early seems like the minimum margin we need.

Homework

- Continue monitoring in the anger log.

- Choose three scenes from the log (low, medium, and high anger). Create need statements and fallback positions for each one.

- Practice visualizing each scene, using RCR response #1 successfully. Start with the low-impact scene and progress to a high-impact scene. Practice the visualization daily.

- Memorize RCR active responses #2 and #3.

SESSION EIGHT

Healing the Shame

Stage One: Understanding

Patience – Healing Shame is a Process

Full Awareness of Your Shame

Explore Your Defenses Against Shame

Explore the Sources of Your Shame

Accept your Shame as Part of the Human Condition

Second RCR Response: Negotiate

Visualization

Third RCR Response: Self-Care

Homework

Healing the Shame

Stage One: Understanding

This time he caught himself before much damage was done. He usually makes up an excuse and runs away as soon as he feels any shame. Sometimes he leaves without knowing what is bothering him and only later connects it with shame. But today he noticed right away that he was overreacting to one small put-down. Then he could remind himself not to flee. He didn't let one small criticism become a total humiliation in his mind.

"I'm finally learning to appreciate my shame. I used to be terrified of it. Now I can sit quietly with my shame some of the time. I try to listen to what my shame tells me about myself, about how I want to live my life. The most important thing I've recognized is that shame is part of me. If I hate my shame, I'm hating myself."

Shame drives down a person's head and eyes. Shame steals energy, optimism and excitement. Nevertheless, the person whose face flushes with shame is also someone who wants and needs to learn how to hold her head up in calm dignity and realistic pride. That is the message of hope that lies hidden in every moment of shame.

Patience – Healing Shame is a Process

Shame is about a person's identity as a human being. Since the wounding from shame is frequently deep and long lasting, it will take time to feel better. The recovery from shame is a gradual process not a one-time event. You might feel terrible one day, better the next, and maybe awful again on the third.

Impatience is a problem as you deal with shame. You naturally want relief from that feeling as quickly as possible. Furthermore, just reading and thinking about shame can temporarily seem to intensify the problem. Above all, you need your shame to go away so that you can feel your right to exist in the world.

A real danger lies in shaming yourself even more by rushing off too quickly to 'fix' your shame. Remember that you cannot force liking or respecting yourself. Self-care has to build gradually. Shame can be replaced with dignity and pride but only slowly. Someone who tries to heal his shame too rapidly may only add another 'failure' to his list.

At first there may be more bad days than good. But after a few months or perhaps a year or longer, you may discover that you respect and appreciate yourself much more than when you first began to heal your shame. The gift of love for yourself is the payoff for dealing with shame and self-hatred.

Full Awareness of Your Shame

Shame is not easy to face. After all, who wants to explore exactly how one holds oneself in contempt? Many people dread the terrible feelings of self-hatred that lie deep inside them and are embarrassed to admit that they have such thoughts. Healing your shame will take courage. You will have to examine your shame even though your natural impulse is to hide from it.

How do you improve your awareness of shame? Completion of this Workbook and following the exercises and homework assignments is the best start. More specifically, notice the messages your body gives you. Clues that shame is present include blushing, looking down, and sudden loss of energy – rapid deflation of the self. You should also listen carefully to your thoughts, especially the automatic insults you give yourself. You can also detect shame in your actions. If you isolate yourself from others or withdraw verbally or emotionally, you may be feeling shame. Perhaps you feel paralyzed (inability to either approach or retreat from a situation because of overwhelming self-consciousness), perfectionistic, or especially criticized by people around you.

Still another way to improve your awareness of shame is to explore you spiritual connections and disconnection. How do you find meaning in your life? When do you feel less than fully human?

Shame episodes can be small or great. If you have committed yourself to becoming fully aware of your shame, you will need to notice the smaller shame events, especially those repeated regularly. Shame can become a habit when smaller shame events go unchallenged.

Explore Your Defenses Against Shame

Earlier, you learned that excessively shamed people often develop survival strategies that lessen their awareness of shame. These defenses minimize the immediate pain at the cost of ignoring reality. Think about the common defenses against shame that you may be using.

Denial – denying the parts of life that bring us shame, forcing our real problems out of our consciousness.

Rage – driving others away so that they cannot see our defects. This is most likely to occur if we believe others are deliberately trying to humiliate us.

Perfectionism – trying to hold off shame by striving to never make a mistake and do everything perfectly.

Arrogance – acting superior to everybody or insisting that others are full of defects. (Arrogance has two parts: grandiosity and contempt)

Exhibitionism – making a public display of a behavior we would prefer to hide. For example, if we cannot read well, we might call special attention to it in a flamboyant way, perhaps by convincing ourselves and others that it does not bother us.

The goal here is to understand how you protect yourself from painful shame feelings and thoughts, not just to get rid of your defenses. Eventually, you will be able to make choices about how to defend yourself. For example, if you habitually withdraw from others when you start to feel shame (or when you fear that you could start to feel shame), you should not feel obligated to stick around and work through shame issues in public. You have the right to stay or leave, depending on what you can handle at the time.

Explore the Sources of Your Shame

It is valuable to sort through the various sources of your shame because each leads to different healing strategies. For example, if your main problems with shame come from living with an arrogant and demeaning partner, your healing will require a different approach than if your feelings of shame have primarily come from childhood. Many persons discover that their shame is related to several sources.

Accept your Shame as Part of the Human Condition

The understanding phase of resolving shame ends when you accept yourself as a human being that occasionally feels ashamed. Your shame will not go away by your fearing, hating, and fighting it. In fact, it could even grow stronger if you fight it. A person who despises his shame forgets that he is detesting himself in the process.

You must accept your shame before you can change it. That is a reality. Shame cannot simply be wished away because it is painful. Nor can it be willed away through being tough. It is far better to befriend your shame than it is to treat it with dread or hatred. All of us feel ashamed of ourselves occasionally. Try to make peace with that shame if possible, because it is really another part of you. We must respect every part of ourselves, including our shame, to discover our love of ourselves.

Review Homework

Review successes from the anger log. How did the visualization homework go? Did you have any difficulty in imagining asking for what you want? Remember that this is just the first of six RCR responses, and that it will be effective in only some of your anger situations. Again, return to the theme of asking for what you want, and remember the importance of putting needs into words.

Second RCR Response: Negotiate

1. Review opening line:

   "What would you propose to solve this problem?"

2. Rules.

   a. If you get resistance or a worthless proposal, offer your fallback position.
   b. If you hear a proposal that has possibilities, begin negotiation. Look for compromise. Examples of compromise options include:
      - "Let's split the difference."
      - "Try it my way for a week. If you don't like it, we'll go back to the old way."
      - "My way when I'm doing it, your way when you're doing it."
      - "We'll do this one my way, but we'll do ___ your way."
   c. Compromise can only be reached when the solution takes into account *both* people's needs.

Read the following *Role Play* between George and his therapist:

George: (provocateur) Stop hassling me about my radio! You make enough noise blabbing all day to your friends. Music is the only way I can stand this job.

Therapist: What would you propose to solve the problem?

George: For you to stop being so tight assed.

Therapist: (fallback position) I just can't think with it on. I'd like you at least to keep it off in the morning when I do most of my writing. How about that?

George: Why don't you buy me a Walkman? That would solve your problem.

Therapist: (looking for compromise) How about if I split the cost of a Walkman with you? How would that feel?

83

3. Visualization.

Select a scene from your anger log in which you feel there is room for negotiation and compromise. Imagine a successful resolution after you offer a compromise suggestion.

Third RCR Response: Self-Care

1. Review opening line:

If {the problem} goes on, I'll have to {self-care solution} in order to take care of myself. This is an exit response. If there continues to be no progress toward agreement, you can stop the discussion here.

2. Rules.

   a. The self-care solution should have as its main purpose the role of *meeting your needs,* not hurting the other person. This isn't something you do to the other person, it's something you do for yourself.

   b. This is your way of solving the problem yourself, not a pushy ultimatum, and not a punishment.

   c. Examples of self-care solutions:

   "I want to be on time, so if you're late, you'll have to go on your own."

   "If you can't help with laundry and housework, I'm going to hire a maid."

   "Jimmy if your clothes aren't on when I'm ready to leave, you'll just have to go out in your underwear and get dressed in the car."

   "Okay you really don't want to do anything tonight. If you're too tired to go out, I'll go with Jennifer."

Homework

- Continue monitoring in the anger log.

- Identify low, medium, and high-anger scenes, as well as appropriate self-care solutions for each.

- Practice visualizing the negotiation of a compromise settlement. Imagine making a self-care statement for each scene. Emphasize that each visualized scene should end in success. Ideally, visualization practice should be done daily.

- Memorize RCR response #4 on pg 93.

SESSION NINE

Healing the Shame

The Action Stage

Get help – you don't have to do this alone

Challenge the shame

Set positive goals based on humanity, humility, autonomy, competence

The Principle of Humanity

The Principle of Humility

The Principle of Autonomy

The Principle of Competence

Take mental and physical action to move toward those goals

Example of an appropriate goal statement

Fourth RCR Response: Get Information

Fifth RCR Response: Acknowledge

Sixth RCR Response: Withdrawal

Homework

Healing the Shame

• The Action Stage

"All I want to do is join the human race. Why is that so hard? What can I do to feel that I belong? Every time I am around people, I just want to run away. I'm so afraid of rejection that I stay home all day."

He yearns to become more independent. But he doesn't know exactly what independence means. Would he have to do everything on his own? Could he ever ask for help? He has spent so much time pleasing others that he is no longer sure about who he is or what he believes in. He feels ashamed every time he depends on others, but he also feels too weak to stand up on his own.

"I'm tired of failing. I'm tired of expecting that I will mess up anything I touch. How can anyone feel proud when they have a built-in assumption of inadequacy? I have got to start taking responsibility to do things well."

Shame is a messenger, telling you that there is something wrong in your life that you must change. You need to pay attention to that message and then take action that will help you live a better and more meaningful life.

Let's look at the five step process to help convert painful shame into positive behaviors. These five steps center on the creation of positive goals, rather than the elimination of shame.

1. Get help – you don't have to do this alone.

2. Challenge the shame.

3. Set positive goals based on humanity, humility, autonomy, and competence.

4. Take mental and physical action to move toward those goals.

5. Review your progress regularly.

Get help – you don't have to do this alone

Isolation is a common reaction to feelings of shame. The more deeply a person is shamed, the more he will hide his thoughts, feelings, and actions from others. People who are shamed keep vast areas of their lives a secret because they believe that others would scorn them if they knew who they really were. Unfortunately, shame prospers in secrecy. By concealing his identity, the person who is deeply shamed only convinces himself that he is fundamentally defective.

But much of shame develops and grows through our relationships with others. That shame can best be addressed when we come out of isolation and communicate with others. Damage from shame begins to heal when that shame is exposed to others in a safe environment.

Not every person can be trusted with your shame. Above all, a trustworthy person is one who will not add to your shame or humiliation when he/she is given private information. Because you may have difficulty talking about yourself, you need to make a commitment to reach out to others at the very times when you feel least acceptable. You need to move toward others even if you are terrified of rejection. At the same time you need to protect yourself by seeking nonshaming persons with whom to share, so your acts of courage will not be met with damaging attacks. (*Note:* nobody can respond to you every time with care and compassion.)

Challenge the shame

Each source of shame must be challenged a little differently. For example, a depressed woman might need to tell herself all five of the following statements at some time during her recovery from excessive shame.

- *That's my depression telling me I'm no good. I can't stop that from happening now, but I know it's not true.*

- *My parents told me I was worthless and I believed them. Now I'm an adult and I can refuse to accept those messages any longer. I think I'll give back that shame because it doesn't belong to me.*

- *My partner criticizes me ten times a day. It's time for me to tell her clearly that I won't keep living that way. I'm worth more than that.*

- *I'm tired of hating myself. For one thing, I'm going to make a commitment not to call myself terrible names anymore. I need to treat myself with respect.*

Set positive goals based on humanity, humility, autonomy, and competence

Four principles are especially significant in this process:

- *The Principle of Humanity*

Everyone belongs to the human race. There are no exceptions. There are no examinations to pass, no duties to accomplish, no possible way to be disqualified. All people are human, and no amount of shame can take that away.

- *The Principle of Humility*

All human beings are equal – no person is better or worse than another.

- *The Principle of Autonomy*

Each of us has the right and responsibility to decide how to live our lives.

- *The Principle of Competence*

Every person is good enough to contribute some value to the world.

Example of an appropriate goal statement:

I challenge myself to develop the habit of <u>competence</u>. I can replace my shame with realistic pride when I work up to my capacity. But I also know when to stop. My goal this week is to remind myself on three different days to accept being 'good enough' rather than being perfect.

Take mental and physical action to move toward those goals

Shame is a mystery. No simple exercise or plan can possibly cover every part of it. But you can challenge shame effectively by making a long-term commitment to think and feel in ways that consistently move you toward self-respect.

Exercise

First, get at least four separate sheets of paper and label the top of each sheet with a separate principle: humanity, humility, autonomy, and competence. On the left-hand side of the page, write under each heading a list of your thoughts and behaviors that regularly pull you away from these principles. Make a thorough list but don't attack yourself. Then ask yourself what you need to do to change each item, and write down those answers next to the original ones. Next, choose no more than one or two things you would like to change. Start with ones that are fairly simple and clear. Finally, commit yourself to making those changes in your daily life, remembering that shame heals slowly and that you don't have to be perfect.

Fourth RCR Response: Get Information

1. Review these opening lines:

   "What do you need in this situation?"
   "What concerns (worries) you in this situation?"
   "What's hurting (bothering) you in this situation?"

2. Rules.

   a. Use this response when someone is angry with you and there is something behind the anger that you don't understand.

   b. If you don't already know what the other person's need or worry is, the process of getting information is vitally important.

   Repeat steps 3, 4, 5, and 6 as previously discussed.

Fifth RCR Response: Acknowledge

1. Memorize these opening lines;

   "So what you want is _____."
   "So what concerns (worries) you is _____."
   "So what hurts (bothers) you is _____."

   Acknowledgment should always follow the information gathering response. Hearing the other person's concern is an important step in de-escalation.

2. Rules.

   a. Use the fifth response when someone has given you a clear message about his or her feelings.

   b. Expect the other person to correct or modify what you said if you didn't get it right. Then reacknowledge the new information.

c. Acknowledgment is not just to let people know you hear them. It is a way to clarify and correct your misconceptions.

Repeat steps 3, 4, 5, and 6 as previously described.

Sixth RCR *Response: Withdrawal*

1. Memorize this opening line:

"It feels like we're starting to get upset. I want to stop and cool off for a while."

This is an exit response. It means that you must be committed to immediately stopping the interaction at this juncture.

2. Rules.

a. Keep repeating yourself, like a broken record, if you encounter resistance. Acknowledge the other person's desire to keep the discussion going, or acknowledge his or her general distress, but keep repeating your withdrawal statement.

b. Physically leave the situation. Don't just leave the immediate vicinity, really get away.

c. With intimates, give a specific time at which you will return to resume the discussion.

Repeat steps 3, 4, 5, and 6 as previously described.

Homework

- Continue the anger log.

- Pick three scenes from the anger log (low, medium, and high) and visualize using RCR responses #4 and #5.

- Visualize the same three responses, but now include RCR response #6 (withdrawal). Do visualizations daily.

- Review the opening statements in responses #1-6 each day.

SESSION TEN

Healing the Shame

From the Family of Origin

The difference between exploring the past & getting stuck in it

Locate important deficiency messages you received from your family

Allow yourself to grieve your life losses resulting from these messages

Review Homework

RCR Switching

Homework

Healing the Shame

• From the Family of Origin

"My parents kept telling me that I was lazy and stupid. They told me I wasn't good for anything. But now I'm an adult. I don't need to believe that crap any longer. I can still hear them saying those things to me, but now I refuse to accept it. Just because they gave me a coat of shame doesn't mean I have to keep wearing it forever."

His father was a functioning alcoholic. But he knew something wasn't normal about his family even as a child. His ears burned with shame when he saw his father and mother argue. Funny that his father never seemed to notice and just kept on embarrassing the whole family. Years later, he still carries the family shame with him wherever he goes. He feels another person's shame, and he needs to give it back.

It is as if you carry around with you a set of parents who live inside your head. These parental images might repeatedly remind you that you are defective. These 'old' parental figures may remain in place even if your parents are no longer alive or have significantly changed and no longer shame you in the same way they once did.

The most common kinds of behavior that produced shame from the family of origin are:

- Messages that you are not good, not good enough, not lovable, or that you do not belong or shouldn't exist.

- Threat of abandonment, betrayal, neglect, and disinterest

- Physical and sexual abuse

- Keeping secrets

- Parental perfectionism

Difference between exploring past & getting stuck in it

The goal in exploring your past is to discover how events have damaged you, so that you can change your current thoughts, feelings, and actions. While you are 'researching' you shame, you will feel pain. But it is important that you work through the hurt rather than get stuck in it. You must bring your head as well as you heart with you, maintaining at least some emotional neutrality to balance your suffering.

Try not to exaggerate events as you explore the past. Probably no parent <u>always</u> shamed his or her children. See if you can recall some times when your parents or other family members praised you, helped you, and clearly appreciated you. Remember that you are dealing with people, not monsters. Ultimately, your shame must be kept in perspective to lessen the risk of getting caught up in the past.

The more deeply you have been shamed, the harder it will be to unglue yourself from previous disappointments, traumas, and abandonment. As you explore the cave of your past, let your friend or a therapist be your rope, and let your commitment to a healthy present be your flashlight.

Deficiency messages you received from your family

The most important deficiency messages are those that affected you the most deeply. These statements might feel correct when you say them to yourself. *Yes, my father always called me a dummy. But he was right. I am stupid.* The messages are painful, and they seem fixed forever.

Write down three important deficiency messages:

    1.

    2.

    3.

It is helpful if you can remember specific incidents from your childhood that involved these deficiency messages. Perhaps you were called clumsy or lazy by a parent as you did chores. Perhaps a parent would no longer touch you after you reached puberty. The incidents may be powerful or small, repeated regularly or occasionally.

Grieve your life losses resulting from these messages

Deficiency messages and other shaming behaviors profoundly affect the developing child. A child who receives deficiency messages will have many needs that go unmet. The recovering adult must grieve these unmet needs. Here are a few examples of deficiency messages:

- 'not good'
- 'not good enough'
- 'you don't belong'
- 'you are not lovable'
- 'you should not exist'

All children want to hear that they are loved, that they belong, they are good enough just the way they are, and that they are totally acceptable to their family. They need to be assured that they are human, normal, and competent. These reasonable needs are not met in habitually shaming families.

Some losses can never be replaced. No amount of praise or respect in adulthood can compensate for the lack of praise or respect received as a child. That is why mourning is a necessary part of healing shame. You must mourn the parts of you that seemed to die in the face of rejection.

Grieving helps you realize that shame attacks the spirit. When we face losses resulting from shame, we feel a penetrating sorrow that can fill us with pain. But this grief can relieve shame when it is experienced fully. It helps us to put away the past, with its lost hopes, so we can find a new path in the future.

Review your Homework from last session

Review anger log, problems, and successes. Review homework. Memorize the responses, because the next week's homework will involve practicing RCR in real situations.

RCR Switching

Now it's time to emphasize the core principle of RCR switching. Try new adaptive responses if anger and conflict continue. Here are the rules for switching.

The following rules will help you learn how to shift successfully from one RCR response to another as you cope in a provocative situation.

All of the lines must be memorized to the point where they can be recalled without effort.

1. Whenever possible, rehearse in advance active response numbers one and three. Decide if you wish to include your feelings about the situation. Then formulate your request and your Fallback position. Make sure it's behavioral and specific. Also try to generate a self-care response. Ask yourself how you can take care of the problem *without* the other person's cooperation.

2. Continued anger or escalation is your signal to *switch* responses. Don't get stuck if a response isn't working. Moving on to what you feel, intuitively, is the next best option.

3. Don't be afraid to repeat responses. You may wish to return, several times, to questions that get more information. You may wish to acknowledge what you're learning about the other person's experience. As the discussion progresses, you may wish to invite another round of negotiation.

4. If you don't know what to do next, try shifting from active to passive responses (or vice versa). If you've been focusing on getting information, try expressing your own needs. If you're stuck in fruitless negotiation, consider asking for information.

102

5. As a rule, start with active response one (ask for what you want) when you're angry or want something changed. Start with passive response four (get information) when the other person is angry and on the attack.

6. Keep shifting among responses until the problem feels resolved or further communication feels pointless. If you're still angry and stuck, go to one of the exit responses (either self-care or withdrawal).

Use the following two coping thoughts whenever a response isn't working and they need to switch:

1. Take a deep breath and relax.

2. I have a plan to cope with this. What's the next step?

Read the following *Role-Play* between Sheila and her Anger Group:

Larry: (provocateur) Why don't you spend more time with your kids and less time trying to raise money for all these big causes, all this political stuff?

Sheila: (trying response 1) You're my brother. I feel really put down and hurt when you say things like that. What I'd like is for you to ask me, if you don't approve, why I do things – not just pass judgment.

Larry: It's all stupid, Sheila. You're wasting your time.

Therapist: Could you try your fallback position, Sheila.

Sheila: Larry, could we just agree to say nothing then? Just leave it alone rather than hurt each other?

Larry: You like to run away from the truth, Sheila.

Sheila: (trying response #4) What's worrying you about my political activities?

Larry: The kids look stressed, they're cranky. They seem a lot more aggressive than they used to be.

Therapist: Could you try acknowledging that?

Sheila: So what's worrying you is that they need to see me more, that they aren't getting enough attention?

Larry: Yeah. And it's affecting their behavior. Frankly, they're turning into brats.

Sheila: (explosively) Brats?

Therapist: Remember to take a deep breath and relax.

Sheila: Okay, this is what drives me nuts.

Therapist: Remind yourself that you have a plan for coping. What should you switch to next?

Sheila: (trying response #1 again) I really feel hurt when you say that. What I'd like is to assure you that I'll think about what you've said. But I'd also like an acknowledgment from you that you know I care about my kids and that it's hard to balance parenting with trying to do something in the world.

Therapist: The request seems a little vague. How do you want Larry's behavior toward you to change?

Sheila: I want to hear what he's noticing about my kids without the heavy judgment.

Therapist: How can you put that into a request?

Sheila: I want to hear what you notice about the kids, but I'd like you to say it without judging the other stuff I do.

Larry: But the "other stuff" is the problem, Sheila. You don't want to face that.

Sheila: This is too much!

Therapist: A deep breath…maybe an exit response?

Sheila: Like self-care?

Therapist: Have you thought out a self-care response yet?

Sheila: I could tell him I don't want to discuss my work again. And if he brings it up, I'll simply stop the conversation and walk out.

Therapist: Try it.

Sheila: I don't want to discuss my political work. Let's drop it. If we get into this again, I'm just going to take off.

Therapist: This is a good place to stop.

Homework

- Continue anger log.

- Review all opening lines on a daily basis.

- Using the anger log, pick a low-risk individual with whom you've had conflict. Visualize using RCR with that person, and plan out a need statement, a fallback position, and a self-care solution.

- Seek an opportunity to engage in an RCR exchange with that person.

- Results should be recorded in your anger log.

SESSION ELEVEN

Healing the Shame

From the Family of Origin

Challenge the old deficiency messages and replace with positive new ones

Challenge your behavior so it is consistent with self-worth

More RCR Switching

Expressing Negative Emotions - Saying "No"

Homework

108

Healing the Shame

• From the Family of Origin

Challenge the old deficiency messages and replace with positive new ones

The best thing that can happen to you if you came from a shaming family is to grow up. No matter how terrible your situation, you are not as helpless and dependent as you were as a child. As an adult you can challenge the bad messages you received as a child. You may have had little choice about accepting these messages before, but you can replace them now with much healthier ones.

Remember these messages originated outside of you. They may have been sitting inside your head for years, but they did not begin there. You can sort through the messages you received in childhood and consciously decide to throw some out. When you challenge the shaming messages you received as a child, you can take the following steps:

- First, identify each specific shaming message

- Second, identify the person or persons who sent each message

- Third, challenge the idea that the message must be true

- Fourth, consider the message and accept or reject it

- Fifth, substitute new, positive non-shaming messages for the old, shaming ones.

Challenge Exercise

1. *Identify 3 - 5 shaming messages*

2. *Identify the person or person(s) who sent each message*

3. *Challenge the idea that each message must be true*

4. *Consider each message and accept or reject it*

5. *Substitute new, positive non-shaming messages for the old, shaming ones*

Challenge your behavior so it is consistent with self-worth

The hard work described in the preceding section pays off when you change your actions to live a less shame-focused and more healthy life. This new behavior may begin with acquaintances, friends, and more intimate relationships. Eventually, though, you will have to alter your behavior with your family of origin or with others who substitute for your family (such as 'authority figures.')

Shame that originated in your family heals best when you change your interactions with your family or family substitutes. Parents do not have a right to shame their children just because they are parents. "Dad," you might say, "you have called me an airhead for years, I'm not an airhead and I've never been one. Please don't use that term again."

These confrontations will not be easy. They will probably be met with angry and defensive tactics, especially if the shame attack is intentional. The best challenges to a shaming family are those that are presented calmly and clearly. They may also have to be repeated regularly, because shaming families tend to return to old, shaming behaviors out of habit.

Some family members or their substitutes can change, and some will do so fairly quickly once they learn that you insist on fair treatment. Others may change reluctantly or not at all. You will have to decide how much time and energy you will devote to the task of changing your family interactions.

Review your Homework from last session

During this week, remember the relaxation and cognitive coping skills learned earlier. Remember to switch back to old responses that have already been tried. You can acknowledge, negotiate, or ask for what you want more than once. As you become more proficient at RCR, begin using medium, then high-impact anger scenes from the anger log.

More RCR Switching

<u>Review</u> this *Role-Play* (as previously read):

Larry: (provocateur) Why don't you spend more time with your kids and less time trying to raise money for all these big causes, all this political stuff?

Sheila: (trying response 1) You're my brother. I feel really put down and hurt when you say things like that. What I'd like is for your to ask me, if you don't approve, why I do things – not just pass judgment.

Larry: It's all stupid, Sheila. You're wasting your time.

Therapist: Could you try your fallback position, Sheila.

Sheila: Larry, could we just agree to say nothing then? Just leave it alone rather than hurt each other?

Larry: You like to run away from the truth, Sheila.

Sheila: (trying response 4) What's worrying you about my political activities?

Larry: The kids look stressed, they're cranky. They seem a lot more aggressive than they used to be.

Therapist: Could you try acknowledging that?

Sheila: So what's worrying you is that they need to see me more, that they aren't getting enough attention?

Larry: Yeah. And it's affecting their behavior. Frankly, they're turning into brats.

Sheila: (explosively) Brats?

Therapist: Remember to take a deep breath and relax.

Sheila: Okay, this is what drives me nuts.

Therapist: Remind yourself that you have a plan for coping. What should you switch to next?

Sheila: (trying response 1 again) I really feel hurt when you say that. What I'd like is to assure you that I'll think about what you've said. But I'd also like an acknowledgment from you that you know I care about my kids and that it's hard to balance parenting with trying to do something in the world.

Therapist: The request seems a little vague. How do you want Larry's behavior toward you to change?

Sheila: I want to hear what he's noticing about my kids without the heavy judgment.

Therapist: How can you put that into a request?

Sheila: I want to hear what you notice about the kids, but I'd like you to say it without judging the other stuff I do.

Larry: But the "other stuff" is the problem, Sheila. You don't want to face that.

Sheila: This is too much!

Therapist: A deep breath…maybe an exit response?

Sheila: Like self-care?

Therapist: Have you thought out a self-care response yet?

Sheila: I could tell him I don't want to discuss my work again. And if he brings it up, I'll simply stop the conversation and walk out.

Therapist: Try it.

Sheila: I don't want to discuss my political work. Let's drop it. If we get into this again, I'm just going to take off.

Therapist: This is a good place to stop.

Expressing Negative Emotions - Saying "No"

Learning how to say no and express negative feelings is another important skill you need to develop. Anger Control problems often come from families in which there were inadequate boundaries and limits. Your parents likely tended to be either overly permissive, overly strict, or inconsistent. In addition, it may have been unacceptable to express your negative feelings appropriately. As a result, you were never exposed to the skills necessary to maintain appropriate boundaries, set limits, and express negative emotions. In fact, one way to understand the anger impulse control problem is as a technique for maintaining internal boundaries. Give yourself time to develop more sophisticated self-regulatory mechanisms first.

You have already realized that a major anger trigger is activated when you feel compelled to say or do things that you aren't comfortable with or when you have to act as though you feel something that you don't. You don't feel able or confident about how not to do what is being asked of you, so you do it, feel terrible, and then act out of anger. Developing and refining your ability to say no directly can put you back in control of yourself, eliminating the need to act out in these situations.

Can you think about particular moments in the recent past when they would have loved to have said "no."?

Write about one such situation:

You may feel that "what's done is done". Often you <u>can</u> go back and 'fix' a situation by expressing your feelings to the person who was initially involved in the interaction. No one expects that you'll always express yourself perfectly the first time. Most people are willing to hear you out, even if it's about something that happened quite a while ago. You can achieve two benefits from doing this. First, you might very well resolve a conflict with someone and feel better about him or her and yourself. Second, by practicing going back and resolving old grievances, you will gradually develop the ability to confront issues as they happen.

Homework

- Use the same homework assignment as in Session 10. Pick at least medium-risk individuals and situations as targets for your RCR practice. Continue to record results in the anger log.

- Continue anger log

- Review all opening lines on a daily basis

- Say "No" on three separate occasions during the week

SESSION TWELVE

Healing the Shame

From the Family of Origin

Return 'borrowed shame'

Consider forgiving so you can be released from your shame

Review Homework for the last time: Saying "No"

Relapses

Ending: A New Beginning

Summary

Evaluation

Healing the Shame

From the Family of Origin

"Here's what scares me the most: Yesterday I heard myself shaming my kids in exactly the same way my parents shamed me. For a few minutes I became what I swore I would never be – an impatient, disrespectful, unappreciative parent. Will this go on forever?"

Return 'borrowed shame'

Shame is contagious in shaming families. It can easily pass from one family member to another, finally affecting everyone. Sometimes one or more persons will gather the shame that belonged to another family member. This shame is transferred from its rightful owner to more vulnerable people.

This shame is called 'borrowed.' The goal is to focus on the possibility of returning it to its original owner. The idea is that, at one time, a person was "loaned" shame against his or her will. This shame originated from the behavior or attitudes of another, usually more powerful, family member. Now, this shame must be returned before the healing person can embrace a nonshaming view of herself. All that is meant by returning borrowed shame is letting others take responsibility for their own behavior or feelings.

Transferred shame may be given to a specific family member either intentionally or unintentionally. Often, it happens when the family cannot stand the humiliation of the real problem. For example, it is far easier to blame and shame a child than to cope with a father's drunkenness. ("You ought to be ashamed of yourself young woman. If you got better grades and caused less grief around you, your father wouldn't get so upset and have to drink.")

Certain children may be blamed the most for family troubles. But others in the family may also 'borrow' shame. Other children are held up as examples and will collect shame and guilt when they fail to keep everybody happy and everything perfect. Parents can and do feel 'borrowed shame' as well, for the actions of a child.

The key to healing shame received from 'borrowed shame' is in recognizing when you are feeling shame about something that has nothing to do with your actions but results from another family member's behavior. If you are returning 'borrowed shame,' you may tell yourself:

Long ago I took on some shame that didn't belong to me. I thought it was mine at the time. So did the rest of my family. But now I know that I did nothing at the time that was wrong. I'm not guilty, and I have nothing to feel ashamed about.

You can directly communicate your resolve to your family members if some of them can understand what you mean. Or if they continue to insist on shaming you through transferring their shame. The main goal here, however, is for you to return borrowed shame that damages your spirit, not to punish others by insisting that they now should feel humiliated.

Consider forgiving so you can be released from shame

Forgiveness can be quite painful. It may bring strong feelings of rage, hatred, despair, and profound sadness to the surface. These feelings are responses to the unnecessary destruction caused by excessive shaming.

Anger is appropriate during this exploration of your childhood. The anger tells us that something wrong happened. It can provide energy for us to make changes in our thoughts and behaviors. We should be careful, however, that our anger doesn't turn into resentment, a far less productive emotion. A resentful person is someone who is holding on to anger and does not want to give it up and move ahead with life.

Forgiveness is a way to release resentments. The purpose of forgiveness is healing ourselves. Forgiveness might lead toward reconciliation with the person who damaged us or with our memories of that person. Forgiveness may allow us to end a relationship that has been based on pain and resentment and get on with our lives.

Remember that forgiveness is optional. Maybe we feel the wounds we suffered were too great to forgive. Maybe we want to forgive but cannot find the spirit within us to do so. Forgiving has meaning only when we realize that we have no obligation to forgive. In other words, forgiveness works best when it is seen as a free gift that we give ourselves with no strings attached. True forgiveness makes no demand. If we forgive another, we do not necessarily have to love her, reconcile with her, or forget about what happened. A change in attitude is signaled by thoughts like these:

I am tired of resentments. They keep me angry and stuck in the past. They only add to my shame. I am ready to forgive the people who shamed me so that I can get on with life.

Review Homework: Saying "No"

What was it like for you to say "No"?

What did you feel?

This is not an easy assignment for most people. Saying "no" can sometimes leave you feeling guilty particularly when you first start asserting your own needs over those of others. This is a skill that you will need to continually practice.

Relapses

The disappearance of feelings of anger is not the hallmark of a successful or complete recovery. As you mature emotionally, you develop healthier coping mechanisms that take the place of the anger problem. Understand that when your anger control relapses occur, you will have broken through a wall of your own creation that was protecting you. It's not nearly as strong as it was before you crashed through it; so be alert to the fact that you are much more likely to slip again and will need to make an extra effort to review this Workbook.

1. Contact people you trust and let them know about your slip. Your honesty with them will help you be honest with yourself and promote your healing.

2. Reestablish relaxation and stress-reduction program
   - Begin rehearsal by imagining the problem situation, including appropriate coping statements.
   - Identify any significant cognitive distortions that trigger the anger and develop appropriate responses or rebuttals.

3. Rehearse, in advance, any RCR responses that might be helpful in the situation

4. Relapse usually means that you have forgotten to implement some of what you have learned. If anger is reemerging, then you should:

   - Reestablish your relaxation and stress-reduction program.
   - Begin rehearsal by imagining the problem situation, including appropriate coping statements.
   - Identify any significant cognitive distortions that are triggering the anger, and develop appropriate responses or rebuttals.
   - Rehearse in advance, any RCR responses that might be helpful in the situation.
   - Consider doing more significant work with a competent psychotherapist or psychoanalyst experienced in the area of anger and shame.

A New Beginning

You have completed The Real Solution Anger Control Workbook. Your thoughts and feelings have been aroused and you have learned some significant coping skills and concepts that will serve you well if you continue to work at them. This experience has not been easy and you can take some time right now to congratulate yourself for a job well done. You are encouraged to review these sessions frequently because they will have new value and meaning each time you do.

We hope you have found yourself with a reduction of shame and an increased sense of hope and higher self-esteem. Even more, we hope that you will use it to help create a world in which all human beings are accepted without fear. Most of all, we wish you a life that is centered around appreciation and mutual respect. Your process of recovery is a new beginning.

Evaluation

1. What is your overall opinion of this Workbook? (1 being *worthless* 10 being *extremely helpful*)

    1   5   10

2. Which session was the most difficult for you? Why?

3. Which session was the most helpful? Why?

4. Did the Workbook meet your expectations? (1 being *not at all* 10 being *completely*)

    1   5   10

5. What do you think about the organization of the Workbook? How would you improve it?

6. What other suggestions would you make to improve this Workbook?

ABOUT THE AUTHOR

Richard H. Pfeiffer, M.Div., CGP, is Director/Founder of Growth Central, a pioneering mental health provider of issue focused, short term group and individual psychotherapy programs and The Real Solution Workbooks. He is a Nationally Certified Group Psychotherapist, a Pastoral Psychotherapist, and a Licensed Marriage and Family Therapist. His psychological / theological training lay the foundation for his expertise in helping people work through their core conflicts. He is a Certified Pastoral Psychotherapist graduating from the Blanton-Peale Graduate Institute (NYC). He holds a Masters Degree in Divinity from Drew University Theological School (cum laude) and a Masters Degree in Education from Temple University (cum laude) where he served in the National Teachers Corps. Richard is a Fellow of the American Association of Pastoral Counselors (AAPC), and Clinical Member of the American Group Psychological Association (AGPA). He is ordained in the United Church of Christ and has served several churches in the NY metro area. Besides founding and directing Growth Groups he has served as the Chair of the Executive Team of the Creative Living Counseling Center, NJ. He teaches, supervises and consults with other professionals in curriculum development, programs, workshops, and small groups for Binge/Compulsive Eating, Anger Control, Assertiveness, Anxiety/Panic, and Depression and is the author of four Real Solution Workbooks. He has provided psychotherapeutic services to individuals, couples and groups for fifteen years. Richard has great enthusiasm for clinical issues seen through the various disciplines of in-depth psychoanalysis, pastoral psychotherapy, cognitive-behavioral therapy and systems analysis.

Growth Central
750 Columbus Avenue
Suite 9S
New York, NY 10025
212-749-3684 voice
212-7497872 fax
mailto:growth@growthgroups.com
Internet: http://growthgroups.com

124

APPENDIX

ANGER LOG

DATE/TIME	SITUATION	TRIGGER THOUGHTS	EMOTIONAL AROUSAL Scale: 1-10	AGGRESSIVE BEHAVIOR Scale: 1-10

ASSESSEMENT

On a scale of 0 - 10 (with 0 being not at all and 10 being severe) How would you rate yourself?	1	2	3	4	5	6	7	8	9	10
I WORRY ABOUT HOW I LOOK										
I AM CONCERNED ABOUT WHAT OTHERS THINK OF ME										
WHEN I TALK ABOUT WHAT I REALLY THINK, I'M EMBARRASSED LATER										
I FEEL SELF-CONSCIOUS WHEN I'M WITH OTHERS										
I HAVE TROUBLE HANDLING CRITICISM										
I'M AFRAID I'LL BE HUMILIATED IN FRONT OF OTHERS										
I EXPECT OTHERS TO SEE MY FLAWS										
I NOTICE MY OWN FLAWS AND FAULTS DAILY										
WHEN OTHERS PRAISE ME, IT'S HARD FOR ME TO BELIEVE WHAT THEY'RE SAYING										
I DON'T THINK I'M AS GOOD AS OTHER PEOPLE I KNOW										
I FEEL SHAME ABOUT THE WAY OTHER PEOPLE IN MY FAMILY ACT										
SOMETIMES I FEEL ASHAMED AND I DON'T KNOW WHY										
I WORRY ABOUT WHAT I'LL DO WRONG										
I HATE BEING EVALUATED, EVEN THOUGH I KNOW I HAVE DONE A GOOD JOB										
I FEEL SHAME JUST BEING NEAR SOMEBODY WHO'S ACTING DUMB.										